THE CURVE
A PLAYWRIGHTS' TIME CAPSULE

VANESSA BATES
MARY RACHEL BROWN
SUZIE MILLER
LACHLAN PHILPOTT
KATIE POLLOCK

GRIFFIN THEATRE COMPANY

CURRENCY PRESS
The performing arts publisher

Critical Stages Touring

CURRENCY PLAYS

First published in 2021
by Currency Press Pty Ltd,
PO Box 2287, Strawberry Hills, NSW, 2012, Australia
enquiries@currency.com.au
www.currency.com.au

in association with Critical Stages

Copyright: *The Curve* © Vanessa Bates, Mary Rachel Brown, Suzie Miller, Lachlan Philpott and Katie Pollock, 2021.

COPYING FOR EDUCATIONAL PURPOSES
The Australian *Copyright Act 1968* (Act) allows a maximum of one chapter or 10% of this book, whichever is the greater, to be copied by any educational institution for its educational purposes provided that that educational institution (or the body that administers it) has given a remuneration notice to Copyright Agency (CA) under the Act.
For details of the CA licence for educational institutions contact
CA, 11/66 Goulburn Street, Sydney, NSW, 2000; tel: within Australia
1800 066 844 toll free; outside Australia 61 2 9394 7600; fax: 61 2 9394 7601; email: info@copyright.com.au

COPYING FOR OTHER PURPOSES
Except as permitted under the Act, for example a fair dealing for the purposes of study, research, criticism or review, no part of this book may be reproduced, stored in a retrieval system, or transmitted in any form or by any means without prior written permission. All enquiries should be made to the publisher at the address above.
Any performance or public reading of *The Curve* is forbidden unless a licence has been received from the authors or the authors' agent. The purchase of this book in no way gives the purchaser the right to perform the plays in public, whether by means of a staged production or a reading. All applications for public performance should be addressed to the author/s c/- Currency Press.

Typeset by Dean Nottle for Currency Press.
Cover image by Adam Nieścioruk via Unsplash.
Cover design by Robbi James for Critical Stages Touring.

Currency Press acknowledges the Traditional Owners of the Country on which we live and work. We pay our respects to all Aboriginal and Torres Strait Islander Elders, past and present.

A catalogue record for this book is available from the National Library of Australia

Contents

Foreword — v

THE CURVE

COVID Love Letter, Mary Rachel Brown	1
The Line Has Been Drawn, Suzie Miller	3
Got You, COVID, Lachlan Philpott	8
Monkey, Katie Pollock	17
The Rush, Vanessa Bates	19
Runaway Train, Mary Rachel Brown	21
Bike Variations, Katie Pollock	23
Habit, Mary Rachel Brown	27
The Fall, Suzie Miller	30
The Last Piece, Mary Rachel Brown	35
East Coast Low, Katie Pollock	38
The First One, Suzie Miller	41
I Can't Breathe, Katie Pollock	47
Are We Happy?, Vanessa Bates	51
Maximised and Minimised, Suzie Miller	54
Nearly Dark, Lachlan Philpott	60
And I'm Here, Vanessa Bates	64
Shine, Lachlan Philpott	66

Theatre Program at the end of the playtext

FOREWORD

In the early days of COVID-19 lockdown in 2020, thanks to a brainwave from Lachlan Philpott, a group of experienced playwrights committed to supporting each other by forming an online writing group to share experiences and read each other's work out loud. There were only two rules: first that we each deliver to a shared Drobox folder a scene that had been written over the previous week—and it could be about anything, as long as it was influenced by that very same week—and second, that we show up online every week to discuss our writing lives and then read each other's work out loud (yes, we the playwrights were the actors in the development—this sometimes allowed for many a giggle).

Write down. Show up. Read out. It seems a simple enough formula but in truth it was anything but. For everyone, COVID-19 has meant different things. It has affected aspects of life, family, social interaction. What did it mean for playwrights? COVID-19 directly affected our creative lives, theatres were closed, commissions were halted, tours of plays we had written were cancelled. For some playwrights it may have afforded time to write, but not if you had school-aged kids or sickness or vulnerable parents. Not if you suffered from mental illness, depression or insomnia, anxiety, creeping fear that the world was about to end. It can be hard to write at the best of times, now it seemed like anything one wrote was at best a distraction and at worst an irrelevance. It seemed as if the whole of Australian theatrical culture had been abruptly cancelled. Worse, it seemed as if we didn't count; the theatre makers, the culture keepers, the artists, the actors, directors, designers. The playwrights. Theatre was the first industry to close in Australia and the last to fully reopen. We were never 'essential workers'. Although we would argue that art and theatre, poetry and literature and music are indeed essential, Australia's cultural life is a reflection of Australia.

With the weight of all this lightly crushing us we began to Zoom weekly, calling ourselves Every Monday. The pieces we wrote and read spoke to how we, each of us (and playwright Ross Mueller who was originally part of this group), felt in this new COVID-19 landscape, how we negotiated our way along stony paths, how we stumbled and got up and kept going because ultimately we knew there was a fistful of playwrights waiting on our computer screens, waiting to hear what we had to say. And there was much to say. Loneliness, fear, bad dreams, repressed attraction or repugnance, lockdown and sudden escapes, jigsaw puzzles, food deliveries, bad tempers and penguins.

The project, given the title of *The Curve*, was supported by the City of Sydney and Create NSW and was our attempt at taking care of each other, and creating a living time-capsule of playwrights' responses to the uncertainty of the COVID-19 pandemic as a genuinely lived experience. We are aware that as residents of Australia we have been so lucky compared to everyone else, and those of us in NSW lucky compared to Victorians, but at the beginning we didn't know this. And anything could change at any moment.

The year 2020 rolled on and the scenes accumulated offering insights into how the pandemic created a new reality and provided an environment within which humans experienced not only the ongoing statistics on risk, illness and death, but a deeper interrogation of what it means to be alive. It seemed that while humour was at times a panacea, it was intensity and meaning that we delved into deeply. Later we discussed at length what we as playwrights could learn from the experience and decided that audiences could be reached in myriad ways that are not always the traditional theatre setting.

With this in mind we explored ways to present our time capsule *The Curve*, and in collaboration with Critical Stages decided to create a filmed version of a selection of the pieces, together with an audio recorded version for radio release, a potential museum installation and lastly a live version performed in a home. When Currency Press and the playwrights' home of Griffin Theatre suggested a hard copy publication it offered a way that the time capsule could be 'buried' in the actual bricks and mortar of a theatre, as well as in libraries or schools—a living record of a shared experience to interrogate and work with, to emulate and to inspire other ways of delivery of theatre to audiences. Later we hope to 'bury' some of the online performances in various websites so that it becomes a community resource of urban and regional playwrights marking this extraordinary period of our humanity, a baton to be passed to future playwrights who are thinking outside the box in terms of supporting each other and interrogating new ways to reflect the Australian community; and an inspiration for future time capsules to be created.

Vanessa Bates, Mary Rachel Brown, Suzie Miller,
Lachlan Philpott and Katie Pollock
February 2021

This text went to press before the end of rehearsals and may differ from the plays as performed.

The Curve was first produced by Critical Stages Touring at FringeHQ Theatre, Newtown, on 28th April, 2021, with livestream and a digital season in the CST Screening Room, with the following cast:

    Kip Chapman
    Laurence Coy
    Katrina Forster
    Aileen Huynh
    Lucia Mastrantone
    Sam Wang

Director, Chris Bendall
Production Manager, Lucy Dinh

For Critical Stages Touring:
Senior Producer, Melanie Carolan
Programming Producer, Emma Corrick
Marketing and Engagment, Robbi James
Creative Producer, Bernadette Fam
Production Supervisor, Judy Reardon
Finance Manager, Kylie Richards

This project was supported by the City of Sydney, Create NSW, the Russell Mills Foundation, and the Australian Government through the Australia Council for the Arts, its arts funding and advisory body. This publication was supported by Griffin Theatre Company.

COVID LOVE LETTER

I'm dressed for it, black and no underwear. I can see you rolling your eyes. Irreverent of me but I am thinking of the little things on this big day. The way you used to pat my dog. Your mouth when you ate ice cream. That double caramel smile. That look on your face when we saw the same thing at the same time, and we just knew. I want to trip you over, send you arse over tit with this knowing.

I want a deep mind-read. Remember those? The gates are still open, run wild, speed, break the law. Drive through the red light of my subconscious. I will pull you over, frisk you and give you a ticket you won't forget. I'll make you pay in desert flowers. Not these fucking lilies. You're a cactus guy.

I want to be the memory that kicks and bucks. Your last rodeo. And you will be my three a.m. wake up. Come join me. Get your ghost on. All the world's asleep, no-one will see you pass through the walls.

How do I get to you? I'll leave the house barefoot, no wallet, no keys. Just the past in my pocket.

Let's load up and go hunting, see who gets the bullet—anger, guilt, depression. Which stage of grief is going to come out of the bushes first? I'm ready to kill. And I'll get you while I am at it. Shoot you a centimetre above the heart, so I can revive you. Flash before your eyes. Be the first thing you see when you come back, everyone else can get in line.

What about time travel? I think it's worth a crack. Let's go through all your ages. We can meet you at the one that included me. I am feeling sentimental. Don't want to be impolite, but I would really, really like to fuck your brains out. Right here right now, in this church. Clock you in the eyes and love you. Dive into your iris, travel to that faraway planet, discover all your aliens. Or we can go local. Just one more trip to the coast would sort us out. A caravan park would do. I am not fussy, you know me.

Don't be shy, let's get all our skeletons out of the closet. I know how to debone. When the job is done, I'll make you a cup of tea. I'll make you a hundred cups of tea, a thousand cups of tea, however many it takes to settle this, to let it all out.

Please do it, sit up and roll your eyes at me. So we can skip this joint, run against the traffic lights on our way to the sea. To that place where the sun clipped you and the tide schooled you in how to return. We could swim out deep to the place where rules and safety disappear. We could hold hands as the water fills our lungs.

It was described in Latin but I could read between the lines. You lay in a landlocked hospital bed and drowned as your lungs filled with fluid. None of us were allowed to be there to remind you that the tide returns and we will never forget you.

Only ten people allowed, but we got quality over quantity. All of us on our knees wishing love didn't have a flip side. All holding it together. All winks in eyes and tears in hearts.

Ignore it. They're wrong. Don't rest in peace, not your style. Riot. Knick an angel's chariot and crash it. Sharpen your wings, get busy, find lightning, wind, fire. Don't tap me on the shoulder, rain down on me. Get in the boxing ring with the gods and make me some thunder. Ambush the seven stages of grief, kill them one by one in front of each other. Make them watch. No turning away. Raise the hair on my arms you beautiful fucking derelict. Let us know we are alive. That's your job now.

They are saying the Lord's Prayer. I am wearing no underwear, did I tell you that? I will miss you forever, dear one.

Mary Rachel Brown
1 April 2020

THE LINE HAS BEEN DRAWN

MAYA:

So, what to tell you. I don't know Lainey, I keep storing up all the details but then when I get to talk to you, they're not the same details. I guess though you're my other half, my twin sister; you have the knowing, that sense of what I am thinking. Do you, still?

So, the flat. Well I ended up getting that new TV and yes you were right. It's way too big, takes up half the fucking living room. And it stupidly makes me miss you being in the flat even more, because every time I turn the thing on, I think, 'Lainey was right, it's a bloody monster of a centrepiece'. I also find myself yelling at the pollies on the news and there's no-one telling me to 'shut the fuck up'.

'Shut the fuck up!' I'm the one yelling that now. At images on an inanimate object.

The flat feels smaller even though I'm the only one here. There's a reason for that I guess. I'm trapped indoors these days. Don't laugh. I know, I know how many times did I say to you. 'You're so lucky being in the flat all day writing, I'd love to sit around in my tracky and not have to put on make-up'. I know you always think I'm insinuating that you aren't working as hard as I am. But ... Okay so I was. I admit it now. To be honest I think if you'd ever had to deal with pre-teens and their fucking parents you'd also think I was right. Now though, these days. I'm doing it your way. In my tracky.

You'll never understand it. What it's like trying to talk to twelve-year-olds on a computer monitor all day. I can tell some of the little buggers are playing games silently on their phones. But what can I prove? Nothing. It's exhausting. But in a different way. So yes. Okay. Maybe staying at home writing all day is harder than I realised.

I hate that you don't live here anymore. There's something about having a twin that is no longer in the womb with me! Remember we always called the flat the womb! It was always the place we went to for comfort, for crying, for ice cream and watching old 'Friends' episodes. I know you remember. You might have moved away but you won't forget those times. The womb! Did you ever tell Mum we called the flat that? She'd probably be insulted. That we'd replaced her. Lol. So, let's make a deal. Let's never tell her okay. Shit she's so fucking competitive about everything.

You will not believe this, but I found that poem you wrote for that old boyfriend of yours, the other day. That young muso guy who needed you to write the lyrics for his songs. Spencer. Was going through some bills and there was a draft of it in the drawer. And I read it. Laughed myself silly. Sorry! You were so in love. But yeah. He was cute. What the fuck ever happened to him?

I was on Tinder the other day. Lainey things are really different now. I now really really wish I'd ended up with a boyfriend in February. I was too picky. Which as you know, is kind of unusual for me. And boy am I paying for it now.

I wander the rooms of the flat, horny as hell. Talking to myself and wondering how I am ever going to have live sex again!

There's a lot that's different all of a sudden.
And it frightens me.
Not the damn virus.
I don't give a rat's about that.
But it's all the, the … difference.
Everyone. Everything.

There's this rule here where you can't go within a metre and a half of another human being. Unless of course they live with you. So I'm fucking done for. I never got around to renting out your room. Your stuff's all in there anyway so I would have ended up with some transient backpacker.

Although Lainey, get this—backpackers are not allowed to wander around either, so if I had rented it out, some Swedish or English hottie might have been stuck here with me. Not able to be within a metre and a half of any other horny traveller. My troubles over.

A metre and a half. Some people say six feet away. Depends I guess on whether you're from the US or the UK, or just here. Which ones still speak in feet?

Six feet away from someone. It's like an eternity.

Because I know when they dug six feet down there. And I knew I couldn't touch you ever again. I couldn't even feel your hair, or smell you, or …

I knew that was an eternity.

But
You know.
The days were weeks were months.

It's not yet a year, and I wanted the days just to keep mounting up. So that, somehow they quietly just came together, and there was some sort of calendar back to you in the flat, sitting on the couch, yelling at me to take the phone into another room.

You and me in this tiny fucking place. The womb. Choreographing our way around each other like parts in a Rubik's cube.

But now.

Now Lainey there's this thing.
This virus.
It's like there's the time before the virus.
And now the time after it hit.
My brain just can't live in both places.

Like now I look at old reruns of 'Friends' and see them all barging into each other's space. Holding hands. Getting in the same car. Sitting around the coffee shop.

And it's like a different planet.
I can't believe I ever thought that was normal.

To not measure six feet away from someone I love.
From someone I know.
From a random on the street.

And there are people dying. Loads of them Lainey.
With no proper funerals.
No-one standing before a gathered crowd speaking long eulogies.

Not like we did for you.

It's like now we have all gone beyond.
Into a different existence. A surreal, otherworldly. Fucking fucked-up science fiction series.

And the big fucking TV at least lets me see all those things up close. And lets me stream Netflix all night every night.

Even if I have to face the twelve-year-olds each morning.
They don't know I'm wearing my tracksuit.
And wouldn't even give a fuck if I was.

And their stupid fucking parents are too busy fighting about toilet paper in supermarket aisles to know how shit the learning is going for their kids.

I'm not kidding you Lainey.
Toilet paper fights.
The Prime Minister.
You don't know him. He's new. He's a fuckwit. I yell at him every night.
But he was on the news the other night and he yelled at all those parents.
Fighting for toilet paper.

And he said.

'Stop it.'

'Just stop it.'

And it was like me yelling at the twelve-year-olds.
Get off your phones. 'Stop it. Just stop it.'

Everything's affected.

A pandemic.
And I'm scared.
Not of getting sick though.
I'm scared because you can't possibly have any idea what I am talking about.
And that makes you feel more than six feet away.
A line has been drawn
And we're on different sides, because you'll never know words like:

COVID-19,
Social distancing,
Flattening the curve,
Shelter at home.

And all these days everyone else is all still here,
Just locked in our homes.
Mum and Dad are at the beach shack.
And me.
I'm here.
In the womb.
Locked in.
Alone.

Suzie Miller
6 April 2020

GOT YOU, COVID

The park. Late afternoon.

JACK, 22, a striking Chinese man, enters. He is dressed in fashionable active wear with a bum bag. He pulls out a plain face mask and puts it on.

Then sanitiser, squeezes a lot of it and covers his hands, face, neck and arms. It burns and stings.

JACK: Fuck. Fuck, fuck, fuck.

> FRANK, *45-ish, stops beside him. He wears a patterned face mask.*

FRANK: Hi.
    You alright?
JACK: It's burning me.
FRANK: Were you in the bushes?
JACK: What?
FRANK: Is that cum?
JACK: No! Who do you think I am?
FRANK: You're young and queer and …
JACK: It is meant to be for sensitive skin. It's fucking third-degree.
    And I would not be doing the beat in a pandemic.

> FRANK *raises his eyebrow.*

> JACK *flicks it away.*

FRANK: Don't waste it.
    Costs more than botox. Or Bollie.

> JACK *is not impressed.*

  Is it easing?
JACK: A bit.
FRANK: Take it back to the shop.
JACK: Thanks for that, Karen.
FRANK: Nice to see you, Jack.

JACK: It guess it must be.
FRANK: Glad you found it.
JACK: So this is it.
FRANK: Do you mean so this is *it* or *so* this is it?
JACK: What?
FRANK: Do you see why I like it or are you going to do your snippy moan about boomers' lack of tastes again?

    JACK *shrugs.*

The sav blanc look again. *Sav blanc is so middle class.*
JACK: Were you quoting me?
FRANK: Yes. What you said in that silly shop.
JACK: Why is that shop silly?
FRANK: Full of hipsters who'd buy anything if they thought it'd make them look good.
JACK: Have you even tried natural wine?
FRANK: I don't care to.
JACK: Boomer.
FRANK: I'm not a boomer, I'm /
JACK: Annoying. Can't be told / anything.
FRANK: I'm Gen X. And that's not true.
JACK: Never heard of Gen X.
FRANK: No-one has.
JACK: Promote yourselves. I could help you if you want.
FRANK: For how much?

    Pause.

Back to the view?
JACK: Ah. The view.
FRANK: Take a better look.
JACK: A better look.

    JACK *looks.*

FRANK: You see?
JACK: Oh … yes.
FRANK: No you don't.
JACK: The way you spoke about it.

FRANK *nods.*

FRANK: You gonna finish that sentence or just do the usual hanging thought?

JACK: You expect more from my sentence and I expected more from your view.

FRANK: You always do.
 You asked me to show you the best thing I saw yesterday.
  This was it. The sun was coming up. The light was catching on the leaves. The lake /

JACK: Pond.

FRANK: The pond then. The pond was sparkling at the bottom of the hill and then I saw the swans with their young, fuzzy little grey things. And they had a duck following them.

JACK: Yeah?

FRANK: Like in the story.

JACK: What story is that?

FRANK: Google Hans Christian Andersen.

JACK: Okay.

FRANK: Not now.

JACK: Sorry.

FRANK: The park was full of dogs without a care in the world, chasing one another, catching and tumbling, and I didn't have to rush to work which made a change.

JACK: Well, I am so sorry I missed all that.

FRANK: You sound it. They don't have a care in the world right now, dogs.

JACK: Were they burdened with a lot before?

FRANK: Yes.

JACK: So carefree they shit wherever they like.

FRANK: Owners are careless.

JACK: People train in this park.

FRANK: Can't miss them, can you? All those double-dipping personal trainers claiming the work has dried up. Everyone is in such a panic about what lockdown will do to their bodies.
 So … how is the share house cold war?

JACK: The same.

FRANK: Caught any of the rats yet?
JACK: No. They're cunning as fuck.
FRANK: Rats adapt.
JACK: We could learn from them.
Since the house meeting, we've kept out of each other's way.
FRANK: You are learning from them.
JACK: At least physically we do.
FRANK: But you hear them like we did when we fucked.
JACK: Yes.
FRANK: Inga's laugh would break glass.
JACK: Ingrid.
FRANK: Oh.
JACK: And yeah, it has done.
FRANK: I don't know how you hack it. Six in that tiny terrace.

  JACK *shrugs.*

They are isolating? You did at least talk about that? Make some agreement?
JACK: Didn't get that far. You should hear Ingrid cry.
FRANK: Jack. How can you know that people are looking out for you?
JACK: Sian uses so much disinfectant I think we'll be fine.

  FRANK *watches* JACK.

FRANK: My offer still stands.
JACK: Yeah thanks but I can't.
FRANK: The cats.
JACK: Yeah but not just.
FRANK: I've got a cupboard full of antihistamines.
JACK: It's your mother.
FRANK: She doesn't mind.
JACK: Did she tell you that? Her house and you've put her in the spare room.
FRANK: Only until /
JACK: Yeah, but it feels a bit weird.
FRANK: Only if you let it. She's deaf as a post.
JACK: All the alabaster flowers.
FRANK: You said you'd help me sell them on eBay.

She doesn't need them anymore. She said so herself. Never collect things.

If you'd just meet her.

The cats like you.

JACK: It's a bad allergy. You saw how I puff up.

FRANK: I'll send the cats to Brian's then you can meet Mum and then /

JACK: I said no.

FRANK: This is about your mum.

JACK: No.

FRANK: She can't tell where you are on Zoom.

JACK rolls his eyes. Zoom.

You want to walk or …

JACK: I don't mind.

FRANK: I brought some wine. Not sav blanc.

JACK: Good.

They smile at one another, slightly flirty.

FRANK: I wasn't sure what to do when we met … how to greet one another.

I mean I knew want I wanted to do.

I saw a couple kissing in the street and it seemed a bit smug.

JACK: We aren't a couple.

FRANK: No. I didn't mean that.

FRANK: I know, it's okay. I'm not needy.

JACK: Good.

FRANK: I do think about you.

JACK: Don't.

FRANK: I hate the nights. Get so restless. Can't sleep 'cause I've done nothing all day but eat. Order all sorts of food online and delivery is such a big event. And then it arrives and gets left at the door and then it is gone.

JACK: Sorted out the kitchen.

FRANK: Me too.

JACK: Got all the baking trays out. Used up all the flour. Cupcakes, brownies, banana bread. All gone and …

They look into each other's eyes. Lust there in FRANK*'s but* *in* JACK*'s* ...

FRANK: Keep thinking about what we did, what I want to do ...
You okay?
JACK: Why?
FRANK: Nothing. Is there something wrong, you look like there is something wrong.
JACK: There's nothing wrong.
FRANK: We're all in shock. And grief. Everyone's grieving, and they're making us carry on as if, as if ... What?
JACK: It's not that.
FRANK: Then what, Jack? You've been a bit ... distant.
JACK: We have to be.
FRANK: What about the couple with the pugs, they weren't? Has something happened?
JACK: No.
FRANK: Did you fuck someone else?
JACK: No.
FRANK: I know we aren't committed so /
JACK: If I'd fucked someone else, I would have said.
It's your mask.
FRANK: My mask?
JACK: Yeah. It's ...
FRANK: What?
JACK: Problematic.
FRANK: My mask?

JACK *nods.*

My mask is problematic.
JACK: It's racist.
FRANK: My mask is racist.
JACK: Stop repeating everything I say, Frank. I have a right to an opinion you know; it isn't an exclusive boomer privilege.
FRANK: Racism is an attitude and this is an / inanimate—
JACK: It's just so wrong.
FRANK: It's a mask, Jack.
JACK: You think it is just a mask? Hah!
Where did you get it?

FRANK: At that conference. They were selling them outside the hotel. Lots of people bought them, even the artists who were there, the Native American dancer asked me for change. We all took photos in the park wearing them, they weren't racist then.
JACK: Wow. A whole bunch of white bureaucrats.
FRANK: I am not a /
JACK: I think that might be subjective.
FRANK: It's was a bit of fun, better than the surgical ones.
JACK: People have said that throughout history, haven't they. Harmless fun playing polo with their heads. Harmless fun /
FRANK: Don't be so black and white. It doesn't dignify you.
JACK: Close down the chinky twink.
FRANK: What?
JACK: Close down the /
FRANK: You think you're a twink?
JACK: I'm just saying that ...
FRANK: Yeah, I've got it. Do you think a Chinese National can speak on behalf of Native Americans?
JACK: Maybe if they are not here.
FRANK: They're very small.
JACK: I saw them.
FRANK: But I mean they'd have small voices so perhaps they'd be grateful.
     The whole tribe might be ...
JACK: It's not a tribe.
FRANK: Oh?
JACK: It's a pattern so it's the same one over. Didn't you ...
FRANK: Black face.
JACK: What?
FRANK: It's not like I'm doing black face.
JACK: Cultural appropriation.
FRANK: Yeah, go and tell all the people in your tute then.

A dog barks in the distance.

JACK: Did you consider any of this when you bought it?
FRANK: When I bought it the smog was so thick, I wouldn't have cared what was on it. They'd been plying us with whiskey because they

thought that's what we liked and they were trying to close the deal.

    FRANK *laughs in disbelief.*

I can't believe we are having this conversation.
JACK: What you are wearing is wrong and you need /
FRANK: Look around you, Jack. Have you ever in your life been in a park where everyone was masked? Where you couldn't see anyone's smile?
The world is slipping out from under our feet. Cling to your undergrad identity politics nonsense if you like but /
JACK: Better than clinging to whatever you hold onto at night with your flaccid cock.
FRANK: What did you just say?
JACK: You heard.
FRANK: You think this virus cares what's on my mask?
JACK: And thanks for showing me the light, Daddy.

    JACK *goes.*

FRANK: Jack? I … Jack, where are you going? Come on, we haven't even …

    He rips off his mask.

I've taken it off. Honestly, I didn't realise it was so … that I was so problematic.

    FRANK *is alone. He gets a bottle of wine from his backpack.*

I even bought this hipster crap for you.
    Fuck it. I'll share it with the chief.

Lachlan Philpott
6 April 2020

MONKEY

WOMAN *at the kitchen table, with a stuffed toy monkey.*

WOMAN:
Cross your legs.

She crosses Monkey's legs.

It's funnier when you do that. Makes you look more human.

She places Monkey's hands on his hips.

Don't be angry with me.

She tilts Monkey's head, cocked at her.

That's better.
I know you can't be angry. It's not in your nature, is it? Not with that giant smile stitched onto your face.
Come on then, put your arms around me.

She wraps Monkey's long arms around her neck so he is hugging her.

See these freckles here? Here on my arm?
Just between you and me Monkey,
I don't think they're freckles anymore, I think they're age spots.
I feel myself getting older every day
but also
—and how is this so?—
time seems to be retracting.
It's quiet above
where there should be a mechanical roar.
The world has dropped away
fallen out of the sky like a bird lying dead on the deck during the fires.
Worldly things are enemies to be feared now
bustle and busy have retreated
and I am left with only myself and my body in space.
And it seems to me

THE CURVE

I am falling backwards
into the essential self of my youth.
Only me.
Bones and teeth inside skin.
No-one to touch.
No-one to touch me.

I am walking down the deserted street of my childhood home
in a world of my own.
Quiet in the sunshine
dreaming.
Hell, you might even say happy.
And out of nowhere appears another girl
Older, bolder, bigger in every way.
An enemy to be feared.

'What you wearing that for,' she sneers at me.
I look down at my frilly white dress.
Broderie Anglaise because it was the 70s and I didn't know any better.
'It's not like it's the middle of summer,' she says.
'Ha ha ha.'

But that's exactly what it was.
England on the twenty-first of June
the summer solstice.
I had no idea.
Didn't even have a watch.

Now, here, under this quiet sky
I feel again that events have overtaken me.
I am separate from them.
The world spins on outside.
Summer, winter, solstice, dawn.
And I'm standing in the middle of an empty road
wearing the wrong clothes
or if they're the right ones it's entirely by accident.
None of it is in my control.
And there is a bigger girl somewhere

laughing
because she knows much more than me.

Last year
going through family photos for the funeral none of us expected
and nobody wanted
there I was
staring out of the album from atop my bed in another country
another time
a hundred worlds before
covered in soft toys.
I drew them close to me for protection
a blanket of friends.
But I see no monkey among the eyes.

It is unseemly for an adult to want a teddy for comfort and company
and yet here I am.

Tonight my human children will return from their other parent
and I will have to give you back.
There you go darling.
Thanks for the loan.
Monkey was good.
He did his job well.
And I'll become old again.

So wrap your arms around me tighter now
please
for one last hug.

Katie Pollock
6 April 2020

THE RUSH

I'm just watching that's all, like anyone, like everyone, minding my own business but keeping an eye.

They're not close to me, not really, standing back at the end of the track, talking to themselves, looks like, whispering, rubbing up against each other and we know that's not allowed is it?

There's two with bushy white eyebrows and that's how you know they're different, not the same as the others. Different, and so in a less civilised setting, they'd have their eyes pecked out.

It's the shoulders that do it, rounded, soft looking, and they rub them against their neighbour and it's hard to see it, emotional, it really is, you know. The shoulders. And the rubbing. And the whispering.

Pretty sure they're about to go, this lot,

about to rush.

I try not to hate them but honestly, it's flaunting really, isn't it?

I note, every now and then, as I turn away, one or two of them look directly at me and that's how I know they can see me, their eyes glint and they're like marbles, glassy and cold and sparkling, hateful, bright with spite, I'd say.

That's what I'd say.

They always look neat and that's a point to them, neatness, co-ordinated.

A uniform of sorts. Monochrome maybe, perhaps dull, but black goes with anything really doesn't it?

And white too.

And finally, they do rush, en masse, towards the camera, head to the keeper with the wet Blundstones and the plastic blue bucket of pilchards, and I say there they go, there they go, there they.

Go.

What time is it?

Change from zoo cam to news cam. Get myself a tea.

I like a green tea with mint although I'm down to my last three bags and that means a trip out to there, foraging, pecking order, wait in line if you don't mind, arms down, feet flat.

And last time, at the fish section, wondering if I should go crumbed or tempura batter and there's a call, and we all look up, all of us, beaks pointed in the same direction, toilet paper you say?

There they go.

And then, moving, as one, not running, god we're not animals, excuse me, excuse *me*, shuffling, waddling, in a crowd, rounded shoulders accidentally touching, pressed against each other, down the aisle, one each, one per person, one at a time. One at a time.

Rush.

And all those sharp beaks.
And all those flat feet.
And all those eyes, shiny, hard, sparkling bright.

Hateful.

Vanessa Bates
5 May 2020

RUNAWAY TRAIN

Mum? Rent? Vet bills? Phone bill? Prioritise! Mum. Visit her before they shut the boarders. Go! Hire a car. Who has been in this car? Sanitise the car. Glen 20 the fuck out of it. Mask! Hand sanitise. Hand sanitiser is so expensive, same as a cheap bottle of vodka ... vodka is on special ... you could ... on credit card. No! Stop it! Get in the car and drive. Drive-time radio, death toll announcements. US death toll overtakes Italy. Drive faster, arrive, wash your hands. Do not infect your one and only mum. Soon as you walk in the door, wash your hands. Did you wash your hands? You do it so often you can't remember, like your mum, you can't remember. Did you wash them? Yes? No? Maybe? There are no maybes! The days of maybe are over! Wash them! Is it twenty seconds or thirty seconds? Is this what it's like to have OCD ... maybe you do have OCD? Explain the virus to Mum, explain it again and again and again. Keep explaining it. Phone call from landlord ... ignore it. Do not tell your mum you need money. Drive home. Drink.

Apply for Jobseeker. Stop avoiding it. Name, age, sex, bank accounts, super, passport number, education—Jesus! Look at the state of your life! Press submit. Reward yourself with Facebook. What are you doing? Watch the real news, not 'crafting ideas for lockdown'. Grown adults doing papier mâché, it's a disgrace.

Do some work! Shakespeare wrote *King Lear* during the plague, so get cracking! Do an online course, too expensive, rip-off! Back to Facebook. You really are a bloody Facebook-addicted disgrace! Other people are homeschooling five kids. You forgot to have kids and now you are alone in lockdown. All your eggs will be gone by the time this is over. You missed the boat, may as well go back to Facebook. Upload ... what should I upload? Anything, make people see you, shine a light on yourself. Let the world know you are alive. Be interesting, suffering, not suffering, good-looking, funny, self-deprecating, altruistic, optimistic, pessimistic—just choose one and upload. Just put a baby photo up there for fuck's sake. Drink, animal gifs, animal gifs, animal gifs—a whole hour watching animal gifs? You are a real-world saver! Check how many likes you got for your baby photo—Twelve?! Stop focussing on yourself. Think of others.

Don't forget the bushfires, the drought, the homeless and the other ones … climate change! What are you doing about that? Do more! Step up. Donate. Work it out. Work out how to be your best self, starting now. Diet, yoga, meditation, declutter. Do home renovations, Google it, you can do it, you can build a yurt.

Zoom meeting—shit! You look like a cave woman! Filter! Smile. Function—technical problems … not really, just need a drink. Zoom, Zoom, Zoom. You are the life of the non-party party. Job well done. Drink!

I really don't feel well. God, I feel distinctly unwell … COVID or hangover? Who can say? Stop day drinking! Get on scales. Jesus, it's like a radio station bandwidth. How do you live with yourself? You must live with yourself. Live with yourself for six months? A year? Some say eighteen months! Two years! So get real! Get relative! Get better at this! Stop eating shit, talking shit and feeling shit. Get out of the house—jog! Everyone is in active wear. Get with the program.

Remember Uncle Bill's online funeral. Don't cry just because you're related, you weren't close, you didn't really like him. You need to like more people when this is over. Don't cry—animal gifs … at the same time as funeral? What have you become?

Wine, Lean Cuisine dinner for one. Text from ex-boyfriend … no—ignore! Facebook, scroll, laugh at Bible bashers, scroll, laugh at Trump, scroll, laugh at God, scroll, laugh at Bondi beach party people. Hate on the right people—What? They threw their pets out the window in lockdown! Don't read it if it upsets you, but stay informed. Give yourself the best chance. Check your super balance— Holy shit! Don't be afraid, it will be alright.

Adapt, pivot. Text ex-boyfriend back, don't send it, just feel the words—don't! Don't even think about masturbating. Hands are for washing and sanitising, not masturbating. Are you masturbating? Can you tell when you're masturbating and when you're not anymore? No-one is watching but your conscious. Wash your hands. Wash your conscious. Get this right. Don't get it wrong. Drink. Sleeping pill. Sleep in. Get up. Do it again. This is no bad dream, this is who you are.

Mary Rachel Brown
5 May 2020

BIKE VARIATIONS

Two limited humans

A: I stand outside my door
B: I wait for my order
A: Might as well wait here as inside
B: Outside with the throng of delivery partners
A: Look at the stars suspended in space
B: Partners, not riders
A: Look at the empty empty sky
B: Not employees
A: Wait for the kettle to boil. Wait for money to hit my account
B: Pretend everything's equal
A: Waiting for something to end. For something to start. Suspended in time
B: Order's in
A: Phone buzzes
B: I load up my bike
A: Pay's come through
B: Check my helmet. Quick kick of the tyres
A: Cold out here so I go inside
B: Turn my bike and ride away
A: Take the rent out first. Then some for the gas
B: Ride and ride and ride
A: And it's time to order
B: Weather's turned cooler. Dark is darker
A: Choose carefully
B: Feel free for a moment. Just for a moment. On my own out here like it's where I'm meant to be
A: Don't be showy, but don't be cheap
B: But it's cold and this isn't my job and I'm not meant to be here at all. I'm meant to be—
A: It's hurt me too, this thing. Just 'cause you can't see the wound
B: I get to the door and the buzz brings me back
A: Saw someone I knew yesterday while I was standing out here

B: Here you go. Yeah thanks. No worries
A: They rode past and saw me. I know they saw me
B: Turn my bike and ride away
A: I saw them and they looked away
B: Another pickup
A: Embarrassed?
B: Another number
A: I turned back inside. Embarrassed
B: Feed the people. Pay the bills
A: Waiting for someone to shout out
B: For this relief much thanks. 'Tis bitter cold and I am sick at heart
A: To tell me to turn back
B: This is my job now
A: But nobody shouted
B: Waiting for this thing to end
A: My order is in
B: No point pretending otherwise
A: Wait now
B: Order in. Load up. Helmet. Tyres
A: Back outside. Look at the stars
B: Wheels on tarmac
A: Be grateful for stars
B: I'm riding it
A: Be grateful for housing
B: Build a wall, look away, kerbside drop
A: Be grateful for the empty empty sky
B: Protect myself, protect my family, feed the people, pay the bills
A: Be grateful for health
B: I'm riding the fuck out of this curve
A: And wait
B: No-one is coming to save us
A: On its way. I should light a candle or something. Lay the table
B: Here now
A: Here now
B: Wait. This is—
A: Hey
B: Oh. Hi

A: How you going?
B: Uh. Guess
A: Sorry. Bad question
B: Here's your food
A: Thank you
B: No worries. See ya round
A: I thought I saw you
B: What?
A: The other day
B: Oh
A: You rode past here. I thought
B: I don't know. Maybe. Probably
A: I just got paid
B: Good for you
A: That's why I ordered. Bit of a treat
B: Okay. Enjoy
A: I hope you like Thai. I wasn't sure
B: What do you mean?
A: I got enough for two. We're allowed guests now
B: Right. Probably why it's so busy tonight
A: It's for you
B: For me?
A: Come in. Eat with me
B: Oh but I—
A: I was waiting to get paid
B: I do like Thai
A: Great. That's great
B: It's really nice of you
A: No it's—
B: But I have to work
A: Oh
B: Sorry it's just
A: Sure
B: You know?
A: No, of course. Food to deliver
B: I'll just turn my bike here
A: Turn that way. There's more space there's more

B: Don't let that food go cold. I rode it fast here
A: Might eat outside. Look at the stars
B: Okay. Thanks though
A: Ride safe
B: Ride and ride and ride

Katie Pollock
25 May 2020

HABIT

'Where do you want to go?' Nice advertising Flight Centre, really packs a punch right now. 'Where do I want to go?' I travel local now, in the middle of the night, without my bags, off I go to the fridge to eat a family-size block of Cadbury's fruit and nut in one sitting. I used to have a habit of getting on a plane and skipping town whenever things got hard. The experts say this could go on for years, so I have taken the time out to make an itinerary of my habits, I hope you find comfort in my sharing.

Habit number one. People call it emotional eating, I prefer to call it what it is, letting myself down and eating too much for my BMI index.

Number two. Watching too much news. Which leads me to habit three. I am becoming sloppy at separating reality from fiction. Habit three-point five, I am starting to believe America is a dystopian overwritten novel that you would not buy even if you were stuck at an airport—I miss airports. I miss lots of things, and missing grows teeth in these times, so I drink. I miss waking up without a hangover. Let's do a combo on the missing and drinking and call them habit four and four-point five.

Habit number five, which is a side effect of habits one, two, three, three-point five, four and four-point five. I have formed a comforting, yet disturbing, addiction to sleeping pills that make me drop things. Habit six, not cleaning up what I drop. I live alone, and I was a grub before all this began, so I give myself permission to ignore broken shit. I accept what I can't fix.

Habit seven, manically buying pot plants believing their growth will be a symbol of hope and wellbeing. Habit eight, forgetting to water the pot plants, which I think is a delayed reaction to habit two, being addicted to the news. Outbreaks of COVID in refugee camps creep up on me when I least expect it, like when I am on my knees beside a dead pot plant. I really shouldn't let Bunnings distract me from my strongest attribute, doubt. Doubt about my capacity to make a difference.

I don't want you to think poorly of me. I have some good habits, even when I don't change my clothes or leave the house for a few days, I keep track of the outside world via the moon cycle. I make a point of looking at full moons from my window. And I make a wish every time one appears. Even when the act of wishing makes me feel like a foolish child, I force myself. Every now and then, in an act of reckless optimism, I buy a scratchy. Because they say 'if the virus doesn't get you the economy will'. Scratchy is as far as my fiscal responsibility goes because I can't, I just can't change my place in this world. This is me, alone and asking the moon for favours at three a.m.

Even though everyone only takes cards now, I always carry cash so I can give money to the lady who begs in front of my supermarket. I have worked out a system, a family block of Cadbury's fruit and nut costs five dollars. So I price-match my guilt and give the lady five dollars. 'The lady'? I should know her name, she is old enough to be my mother. Too old to be on the streets, she begs alongside someone too young to be on the streets. To solve this on an internal micro level, I eat eight rows of Cadbury and employ habit four, drinking.

If you are still reading, I want to try and make this useful for you, everything you have read thus far is just me using my own fallibility to warm you up for some questions you might find helpful. Just tick yes or no and if you are unsure, feel free to tick between the boxes.

1. Are you carefree? If you answered yes, I am happy for you and you can jump to question ten.
2. Are you fearful?
3. Are you angry?
4. Are you guilty?
5. Are you riddled with doubt?

Remember, you can tick between the boxes, especially if you have doubt about your doubt.

6. Do you have debt?
7. Shame?
8. Regret?
9. Lost love?

10. Last question, if one is terrible and ten is excellent, on the spectrum of self-love, what number would you give yourself?

I hope that was constructive for you. If not, take solace in the scratchy I have enclosed. Sorry it is a used scratchy but I could not sleep at night if I knew I was burdening you with any unrealistic expectations. On the upside, it has a two-dollar win on it, so silver linings. You can use your free will and make the decision to cash it in, spend it, give it to someone, or keep the coin in your pocket as a token of luck. We have to keep the economy going. The economy of love. So keep trucking. All the best, and every time you walk past here ask yourself, 'Where do you want to go?' Now more than ever, 'Where do you want to go?'

Mary Rachel Brown
8 May 2020

THE FALL

JESS, *artist, 40s. In her painting studio and painting overalls.*

JESS:
At first it was quite brilliant, a sort of secret six months off;
Autumn.
The Fall.

I could catch up a bit
Be a great mum, cook more, love harder, paint more, less chat, less social stress, more boxes sorted, establish a routine of walking the dog, eating, working.
More fucking,
more everything.

A famous musician friend from London decides he will email a music track a day, to reach us all in isolation.
Connect us.

We are 'all in this together'.
We all belong.

I join a neighbourhood group app.
Share information about where to buy flour.
Stand in my driveway on Anzac Day,
at dawn, with a candle.

I hear birds in the morning,
no planes or traffic to disrupt them.
Calm.

No FOMO while I languish at home because nothing is happening.

Board games are played.
I consider a neighbour's offer to share his sourdough starter,
but then … pah.
I plant herbs.
Unpack old boxes,
find small treasures
each with a story.

THE CURVE

Watch a TV show about people watching TV shows.
Laughing at what we had become.

I watch a new-release film,
right there in my living room.
Make popcorn and a homemade choc top. Bag of Maltesers.
Facebook about it.

At first it felt quite the balm.

At first.

Then it just happened.
Not a physical fall. Nothing literal.

Just this strange dive.
Frantically trying to figure out which way is up.
And down.
And night.
And day.

I watch a series about innocent people on death row.
Thirty years spent in a tiny cell,
then on one random day they get to walk free.

For me it was the doubt that started to creep in.

Yet it started
quite unusually.

The old dog pissing on the sofa.
A memory.
A dagger to the heart.
A four a.m. panic attack.

And then it was *on*.

A sense of impending doom.

I watch a documentary about elephants
but when a baby elephant is left behind
I have to change the channel.

I think about who would be there at my side

on my deathbed,
who would stroke the hair from my face.

This new fall is not about the virus
because the virus is the new normal.

I want to strangle time
freeze the moment and dissect it so that I know it.
So that I can still boil the kettle,
cook fish fingers,
find the bandaids.

Because suddenly I am in the shoes of another woman.
Someone who I don't know.
This new woman,
who are you?
Who are you?

I turn off the news about nursing homes.
And COVID.
Vacantly stream a reality show about how the
exceptionally rich throw parties for their toddlers.
Extravagance.
For what reason?
Because they can.
Because the toddlers deserve it.

Reading through old diaries,
hours, weeks, years of writing.
Exquisite sentences, heartbroken laments.
I like
her.
She was warm and gracious.
No bitterness
just vulnerability.
And such an appetite.

Dived
into sex, life, love, passion, politics, music,
art, adventure

How do I find the me in me?
The her in me?
The person who wrote all those diaries.

I watch a show about building a house from sandstone.
A beautiful house with a singing tower.

An opera singer lives there,
she walks up the spiral staircase,
stands at the tower and sends her powerful voice over the vineyards.
Lush grape-laden vines.

They said that the house was built to outlive those who built it.
To be rediscovered in years to come by new inhabitants.

My childhood house was demolished in a day
and rebuilt into a block of flats in under a month.
Who will find the time capsule I buried under the shed?

I see a TV show about young lovers that runs for hours,
I watch it until there is no more.
It is five-thirty a.m.
I am sick with jetlag
that is not even jetlag
because there are no longer any jets.

I climb the stairs to bed
and as the morning birds start to sing
I put earplugs in my ears and turn morning into night.

It feels that in isolation things don't grow.
The herbs lasted for the first three weeks.
The neighbour's sourdough starter died a bored death.

My musician friend sending a song a day reached his fifty-third
offering
And
stopped.

My boxes of things to sort are all sorted.
My mother's leftover papers, my father's certificates and letters.

And my childhood memories,
my children's childhood memories.
All the boxes are sorted.

What to do with them?

And that house built from sandstone.
Will it be weathered to the ground?

Or
Maybe
a century from now
it will be inspected by a young woman
with the voice of an angel.
There will be a moment.
A connection.

She will
climb the stairs to the song tower,
made of wood sourced from the local area, decaying now.
She will step into the song tower,

open the cracked window,
push her face through

see the long-dead vines below.

    Pause.

And sing them into life again.

Suzie Miller
18 May 2020

(*The Fall* first featured on 'Dear Australia', 2020)

THE LAST PIECE

CAROL *sits a table, she is at the beginning of a large jigsaw puzzle.* RON *is circling her, his attention is split between looking at his wife and looking at the cover of the jigsaw puzzle box. Both infuriate him.*

RON: You know what gets me most about the jigsaw puzzle—
CAROL: No—
RON: The way the end result always matches the front of the box. There are no surprises! You begin knowing your end destination, and that there is the antitheses—the absolute antitheses of adventure.

> *Beat.*

The jigsaw—
CAROL: Alright—
RON: The jigsaw puzzle is a slow crawl towards predictability.
CAROL: Goodnight, Ron—
RON: It's the slaughterhouse of expectation.
CAROL: Expectation can be a burden.

> *Pause.*

RON: Time killers, that's what they call jigsaw puzzles.
CAROL: They?
RON: People who got life right.

> *He looks at the lid to the jigsaw.*

A meadow, a path—Jesus—and a little cottage, there is always a little fucking cottage and a woman with a basket making her way up a hill.
CAROL: This is going to take me several hours so you need to find a way to regulate yourself, Ron.
RON: You're planning on finishing this?
CAROL: This and our marriage. I am going to fill in every little gap until I am done.
RON: Then what are you going to do? Frame it? Look at your act of slow-motion murder and pat yourself on the back. That what you're going to do?

CAROL: No.

> *Beat.*

I am going to start again.

> *Beat.*

RON: Okay, well that is that then.
CAROL: That is that, Ron.
RON: Okay. Well, it is goodnight from me.

> *Beat.*

I said goodnight, Carol Amelia Littlewood!

> RON *drops the jigsaw puzzle lid and heads out.* CAROL *pulls him up.*

CAROL: Ron!
RON: What!
CAROL: You know.
RON: I'm not a mind reader.
CAROL: And I'm not stupid.
RON: Spit it on out, Carol?
CAROL: Give them back; the missing pieces—
RON: I don't have—
CAROL: Yes you do.

> *Beat.*

Give back what you have taken, Ron.

> RON *gets two jigsaw pieces from his pocket and slams them down on the table. He heads toward the door.*

All of them.

> RON *retrieves a jigsaw piece from his pocket and drops it at his feet.* CAROL *get up, straightens her skirt.*

Okay, Ronald Norbet Littlewood. Fine.

> *She walks towards* RON. *They stand face to face for a while.*

Not a problem.

CAROL *bends down to pick up the jigsaw piece.* RON *gets down on the ground, mirroring* CAROL*'s level. They kneel face to face for a beat.*

RON: Please?
CAROL: It's too late, Ron.
RON: Please?

CAROL *picks up the jigsaw piece. She walks back to the table, straightens her skirt and sits back in front of the jigsaw puzzle.*

CAROL: I've made up my mind. I am finishing this, the whole picture, even the very beginning bit where I mistook seduction for love. That's me, the woman on the path, with the basket making her way up the hill, and I am going to get there. I am going to open the door to that little cottage and close it behind me. You're not allowed in anymore. Sleep well, Ron.

RON *exits.*

Mary Rachel Brown
24 May 2020

EAST COAST LOW

WOMAN:
    The east coast low
    brings big swell, big tide, big rain
    smashing down on us
    sheltering
    here inside the eye of the storm

    It suits this downwards pressure
    on money, on jobs, on life
    No jumping up and down in the pub
    No 'Have To Dance To This!'
    No joy
    except in sourdough and small birds

    Remember that night we went clubbing?
    My first on e
    Probably your hundredth
    but you made me feel like we were virgins together
    In and out of the little clubs, little bars
    back and forth across the street
    up the back stairs to rooms of black lit up by ultraviolet light
    Pumping
    Jumping up and down
    and somewhere in the middle of the dance floor
    a moment of exquisite stillness
    watching my hand weave shapes in the sweat-filled air
    Beads of brightness on my hand shining under the ultraviolet purple
    like dust motes caught in a sunbeam
    Dancing
    Dancing
    My hand dancing its own tune
    weaving through the air
    our bodies weaving through the crowd

    Here tonight

THE CURVE

I was set
I was ready
to throw out the sourdough, shut out the birds
to yell out at the storm
Blow, winds, and crack your cheeks! Rage! Blow!
Then
black
quiet
all power gone
And my high voltage condenses to single flame

The air fills with the cloying vanilla smell of candles foraged from
a teenage drawer stuffed with makeup and hope
The east coast low has blown us off target
off course
with its downwards pressure

Did you want to work?
No
Did want to read?
No
Did you want to fuck?
Yes

But you left us a long time ago and some other guy is on his way
over

Bring candles I say
Bring candles and wine
Bring candles and wine and your body
Outside, a dragon breathes out and in and out and—
Inside my head or outside the door, the sound of a dragon, the sound
of pumping beating life

The neighbours will know he knocked on my door
The neighbours, who I know now, will hear him knocking, knocking
the wall, knocking
The neighbours will go to bed early, lights out, candles out
while the east coast low rides up and down our border
pounds on and off our shore

THE CURVE

blows down powerlines, blows out plans, blows our minds
holds us in its grip
tight
tighter
wait

It hasn't finished with us yet

The candle burns itself out
The door clicks shut behind him
A flicker
and then
No! Too bright!

Outside the door a low hum
The dragon has turned away
The east coast low flicks its tail and slinks off into the night
laps the shoreline
The stove light blink-blink-blink-blink-blink-blinks

That night we went clubbing in the purple light
we should have fucked then
like dust motes caught in a sunbeam
like virgins

Katie Pollock
28 May 2020

THE FIRST ONE

LISA:
So hi.

This is weird.
I've never done anything like this before.
I mean not just during a pandemic but even …
You know even online before, I've … Sorry?
Hang on.
My Airpods are in the wrong ears!

She adjusts them.

That's better.
What was that?
Oh, no I said I haven't ever done an online version of this kind of stuff before.

No, nope, never.

Oh okay.
So, okay, so that makes me a little nervous then.

Because that means you know how this stuff works and—well you have an advantage is what I am saying!

Laughs.

Okay so um …
Really you want me to answer? Oh God. I don't know.

I don't know, I'm scared to say because it's probably a loaded question.
Okay um, a dog? Maybe? What, any dog?

Small moment.

Okay. I've got one. But don't judge me!

I'll say, maybe a, a labrador, or a, what are those ones with the …?
Oh I can't remember what they're called so I'll stick with a labrador I guess. A chocolate labrador.

That's pretty good, right? Friendly. I guess it has to be, right? Good. Okay, so I'll take that then. Friendly.

Soo. What about you?

Ohh, I like greyhounds. They're ... elegant. I wish I'd said greyhound now.

Laughs.

Just because it's probably a bit sexier to be elegant than ... I don't know. Oh God. I think I'm going to drink my wine now!

It's here.

Already poured.

Oh, good.

So

Cheers

A sip of wine.

Yeah it's a nice red. Merlot I think. You?

Wow, great. That sounds expensive, and ... elegant!

Laughs.

Exclaims.

Oh. Okay so we're onto serious, are we? ... Well, just two months actually.

Uh-huh.

No. It was kind of sudden. But yeah, it's definitely over. What about you?

No, no, we were isolating together and, and, I don't know it just ...

Yeah fizzled out.

It's definitely done, yeah.

So what about you?

So that was kind of ... long-term. Right. Sure.

Wow.

That sounds ...

Really?
Friends? That's very, I don't know, mature I guess of you both.

Yeah.

No we, we ... no.
Not friends I'm afraid.

Yeah.
Probably it was all too new to think of isolating together. We just got ... I don't know.

Well yeah, bored is one word for it I guess. But—yeah—it was too ...

Yeah right. Too soon. Enough said. Anyway.
So are you still working through all of that?

Great, and what exactly do you ...?

Oh you are? Wow that's very cool. Is it ... do you feel in danger?

Wow it's like you're one of the heroes of this whole thing then.

Still.
It's ... God ... I think it's really brave actually. So what's it like each day?

But they can't have visitors, right?
Oh fuck, what do you say to them?

Really.
That's intense. Are you feeling ...?

No, no, I like it.
I mean, not like *it*, but it feels good to talk about something, I don't know, something real.

Yeah.
No, I was working at a restaurant in the city, and it closed pretty quickly to be honest.

Very.
Mainly because I wasn't sure how to pay the rent at first to be honest. But things got a bit better when Jobkeeper came in.

Well at first I just kind of did stuff around the house and, God, my life feels really ordinary compared to what you just told me to be honest.

No. I'm really glad you did actually. Can I ask you …?

Did the person's mum, your patient … Will she, will the mum recover?

Okay so there's still some hope then? Good.

Fuck.
Who'd go on a cruise. Shit!

Me?
Um?
Well I binged a series called 'Normal People' /

Yeah, yeah me too!
Oh, you mean the one about the guy with the tigers.

No. I can't say I did actually.
Everyone else seemed to be mentioning it on Facebook
But for me it was just … actually to be honest I found it a bit … depressing.

You did?
I know right.
And everyone seemed to think it was *funny*!

I'm glad there's at least one person on the globe that agrees with me then.

> *She sips the wine.*

Pardon?

> *Smiles.*

No, I just thought you said something.

> *Smiles.*

You have a nice smile.

Thank you.

Uhh awkward.
No. No I don't mean it. I was just feeling … I don't know.

That was just a really nice thing to say.
And,
And, I think I meant 'awkward' as in, I don't know, shy.

Yeah a bit.

Thank you.

Harvey?
You're a really nice person.

    She tears up without warning to him or to her.

God sorry. Fuck.
You must think I'm a total—

No I'm fine. I am. I really am.

It's just. Okay. So …
That guy I was telling you about before.
I mean when you asked if we were still friends—

I think isolating with him
Changed me a bit.

Yeah.
He—
There was a lot of—
Well what I'm saying is that,
that he was—

One night the upstairs couple had to call the cops.
And, yeah. He got taken away with them.
I haven't seen him since.

Sorry, I bet you wish you didn't ask.

Anyway, I've been here on my own since then.

And then I guess meeting you is kind of—

God I'm so sorry.

Even I know this is *not* how these things are supposed to go!

    Laughs.

Fuck.
I think, I just … no offence to you, of course. I mean you're …
I just think, I think I need to go now.
But—
Can I ask you …?
Even if you don't really want to follow up on this, this …

Yeah. Date!

Even if you don't want to do this again because after all that over-sharing before, I would fully understand that you wouldn't want—

Oh, that's … thank you.

But I just wanted to know
If.
Even if you change your … or you're just being polite saying—
God I just wanted to know that,
If maybe you might, somehow, just let me know about that girl's mum. The patient from the cruise.
Whether she makes it or not.

And if the daughter you talked about, the girl, if she gets to see her mum again?

Can you just, maybe, text me that information when you know it? That would be …

    She has no more words. Shrugs.

Thanks

    Holds back the next wave of tears.

Okay

    She exits the chat. Closes the computer. Takes her Airpods out.

    Stares.

Suzie Miller
1 June 2020

I CAN'T BREATHE

MARK *and* MUM.
MARK *is in New York,* MUM *is in Sydney. They talk on the phone.*

MUM: Mark? Mark is that—
MARK: Hey.
MUM: Mark?
MARK: Hey yeah, hello …
MUM: Hi can you—
MARK: Hi yeah Mum it's me …
MUM: Why are you—what's what's—
MARK: Yeah Mum I'm just—
MUM: What time is it? What's—
MARK: I dunno it's like—
MUM: It must be, what, about—?
MARK: It's late.
MUM: It must be late.
MARK: It's like ten thirty or, I dunno, nearly—
MUM: Why are you calling so late?
MARK: I was just—
MUM: What's happened?
MARK: Nothing, no it's—
MUM: Is everything—
MARK: No I mean apart from everything, it's all—
MUM: Mark?
MARK: I'm fine. Mum I'm—
MUM: Oh, darling …
MARK: Really.
MUM: It's so nice to hear your voice.
MARK: I just wanted to call. That's—
MUM: Are you—?
MARK: Okay. Alright. Just don't panic or—
MUM: Why?
MARK: No. Nothing. Mum. I'm fine.
MUM: It's so nice to hear your voice.

MARK: It's nice to hear yours.
MUM: It's late darling. You must be tired.
MARK: No I'm good. How are you?
MUM: Oh, don't worry about me.
MARK: I'm not, I just—how are you? How is everything?
MUM: Fine. Fine. Cold! But—
MARK: Yeah I saw.
MUM: Oh, you wouldn't—
MARK: Sixteen degrees! You must be like oh my saints!
MUM: Oh, stop it …
MARK: Pass the double doona!
MUM: Nothing to you now, I know, I know …
MARK: I'm just—
MUM: You know how I hate winter.
MARK: Haha I'm just teasing.
MUM: I don't know how you can stand it there.
MARK: Don't start …
MUM: I'm just saying it's cold …
MARK: Comes with the territory Mum.
MUM: How you doing? How you feeling?
MARK: Better …
MUM: The symptoms are—
MARK: Gone. Really—
MUM: You're not just saying—
MARK: No, I am. Much much—
MUM: How's your breathing?
MARK: It's … it's …
MUM: Mark?
MARK: It's getting there. I mean … I can breathe …
MUM: Wouldn't you rather be home in the sunshine?
MARK: Sixteen! You just said—
MUM: It'll only last a week.
MARK: Ha!
MUM: Well?
MARK: I'm just fine here.
MUM: You've had some trouble …
MARK: Yeah. Man …

MUM: Riots! My god ...
MARK: I know.
MUM: It's been all over the news.
MARK: Has it?
MUM: Even near you. I thought I saw on the TV—
MARK: Oh, that's good—
MUM: That corner where you get your—
MARK: On your news? Wow, that's actually—
MUM: I can't understand it Mark ...
MARK: People are angry Mum.
MUM: I know but—
MARK: Like really fully—
MUM: But why do they have to destroy everything?
MARK: Why wouldn't they? They're so angry and fed up I don't blame them. How else are they going to be heard? They've been smashed by the system, and smashed by this idiot president, and smashed by this fucking virus and now this? A knee on his neck for nine minutes! An unarmed man! It's too much ... it's too—

MARK breaks off into a cough.

MUM: Mark! Mark!

Coughing abating.

Mark?
MARK: I'm okay ...
MUM: Don't get yourself so upset.
MARK: What?
MUM: You shouldn't get so upset.
MARK: Why not? Why shouldn't I?
MUM: It's not your fight darling.
MARK: But it is.
MUM: But sweetheart ...
MARK: If I want to be part of this society I have to decide which side of the line I stand on and then I have to go and stand on it.
MUM: I wish you were here. It's safe here.
MARK: That's why I'm not there.
MUM: I don't—

MARK: It's too safe there. Too easy.

MUM: Oh, come on …

MARK: I mean it. When I'm old I want my wrinkles to be from leaning into the wind, not lying back in the sun.

MUM: We have troubles here too you know. The same things have happened here and we didn't all rush out and burn the place up.

MARK: That's the point. Nobody ever does anything. I'm not like that.

MUM: I know …

MARK: I want to do something.

MUM: You're a beautiful young man.

MARK: Oh Mum, stop that …

MUM: I worry about you.

MARK: I'll be fine …

MUM: I want you to come home.

MARK: I am home.

A moment.

MUM: How are the pot plants? Is that monstera taking over?

MARK: Hey Mum, I've gotta go—

MUM: Oh …

MARK: I just wanted to hear your voice.

MUM: Are you going out?

MARK: Yeah …

MUM: Outside on the street?

MARK: Yeah …

MUM: Do you have to? Mark?

MARK: Yeah. I do.

MUM: Will you at least wear a mask … for me?

MARK: Of course, I always—

MUM: And you can breathe okay with a mask on?

MARK: Mum …

MUM: Mark … can you breathe?

MARK: Yeah Mum. I can breathe.

Katie Pollock
1 June 2020

ARE WE HAPPY?

KATE *is doing a cooking class on Zoom.*

KATE:
Are we ready? Are we happy?
Hello Rosie! Hello Lorna!
Margaret? Are you watching? You're looking off to one side, it's a bit distracting.
Face the front please. Good girl.
Hi Jim! Hello Annie! Now don't be putting me off you lot! Sending me off course.
I know what you lot are like. Now …
Bonjour! Buenos dias!
Good morning!
Hello! Everyone!
Face the screen please, Margaret. That's right.
Look out the window, at that *sunshine*, do we all have sunshine? All of us? Glorious! Oh, okay not you, sorry Jim. Bad luck.
But for us, the ones with the sun!
Glorious!

>   *Sings:*
>
>   The sun has got his hat on, hip hip hip hip hooray
>   The sun has got his hat on and he's coming out to play!

Do any of you know where that comes from?
No Lorna, not 'Play School'.
No Jim, not 'Romper Room'.
No Margaret, not 'The Bill'. That's a bit silly, isn't it? 'The Bill' is a bit more sophisticated. Also, a police show. Why would police officers be singing about the sun? That's right Margaret, you *weren't* thinking.

It's from 'Charlie and Lola'!
'Charlie and Lola'. Charlie and his little sister Lola!

Actually, Margaret, it was a very successful children's television show.

My son used to watch it all the time when he was a tot.
Oh, yours preferred 'The Bill', did they Margaret? Explains a lot.
Anyone's kids watch 'Charlie and Lola'? Other than yours, Margaret, of course.
Grandkids?
Never mind.
How did you all sleep?
Rosie? Good! Annie? Good! Me? No. Dreadful.
Don't mind me. I'll be fine. Little nap later in the day. I'll be fine.
I will. Fine.
So. Sourdough! Are we all ready? Are we happy? Glorious!
Pay attention because …
This is one of those 'no knead' breads.
I said … No knead.
Not need. Knead. No knead.
I know, I know! So exciting. Lorna … Annie … Rosie … Just think of all that time we spend.
As women. With our hands right in it. Flour up to our armpits. Kneading and kneading. And kneading. And kneading.
And now. Turns out …
It's just wasted time really. Need. Wasted time. When you think about it.
What's the point?
Because you put all that work in, growing your kids and cleaning your house and washing your hubbies' clothes and suddenly it's all pointless.
You're pointless. You're just a pointless old lady chatting to her computer.
To all her old lady friends. And one old man friend, yes okay Margaret, sorry Jim.
A lot of lovely friends.
At the Neighbourhood Centre. That's right, Margaret. Don't rub it in.
Oh, you don't want to make sourdough anyway? You think it's boring and it was all done weeks ago. I think you're being negative Margaret. And also I think … beggars can't be choosers. So let's make this bread and let's all be grateful because you don't have to fucking knead it.

THE CURVE

Now, where were we?
Stop crying, Rosie, the flour will get damp.
Trust you lot to send me off course.
I said that, didn't I? Didn't I say that, Jim?
You lot!
Now … We need flour of course! I'm talking about the other need that's right Jim, quite the pedantic old fart, aren't you?
Rosie! Stop crying!
Yeast.
Pinch of salt. And two cups of blood-warm water.
Bowl at the ready? Yes?
Margaret? Looking this way.
Everyone. Looking this way.
Are we happy?
Are we?
Yes?
Good.

Vanessa Bates
27 June 2020

MAXIMISED AND MINIMISED

Two women on an online Zoom chat. They can screenshare as well. (When performed live they can both face the audience.)

JENN: Have you been on all day?
AMY: No, I just jumped on; heard things are hotting up,
JENN: I've been on all day.
AMY: What sitting there all day. With volume?
JENN: No, no volume. It's live at the night in the USA, so I just had it there. I wasn't just sitting watching; I was in my normal day writing my normal reports.
  Had it minimised on my screen—just there; glancing at it from time to time.
AMY: Was that weird?
JENN: Yeah a bit.
  To be honest at times I kind of forgot it was there.
  And then bang you'd glance over and whoa!
AMY: That's freaky.
  Were other people watching?
JENN: It started with seventeen of us /
AMY: Seventeen people watching!
JENN: Well, there were seventeen, sixteen or seventeen of us for the first while.
AMY: That's like thirty-four eyes on your …
JENN: There's a hundred and fifty-two people on right now. Something's up.
AMY: Fuck.
JENN: Hang on a hundred and fifty-seven now and counting.
AMY: Are they all … 'friend' friends?
JENN: I think it's friends and then friends of those friends, or people who heard about it through friends.
AMY: One hundred and fucking fifty-seven!
JENN: Hundred and sixty.
AMY: Of your 'nearest and fucking dearest' staring up your …
JENN: A hundred and sixty-nine now. Numbers are going up.

Maybe we should put it on full screen.
Can you put it on your screen and still talk to me?
AMY: Yeah. I can do that.
God they could sell tickets—wait—are we paying to watch?
JENN: No it's accessible to anyone.
AMY: Oh wow!
All that fucking nakedness. She must have good self-esteem!
JENN: I know, right.
So Dad must have walked past at one stage,
stood behind me and was like 'what the fuck?'
AMY: Shit. What'd you do?
JENN: Well, he didn't actually say that, or anything!
I just quickly maximised my Word doc.
AMY: Huh, you maximised!
JENN: Yeah, I mean, the report I was writing on drainage systems in vertical landscaping.
AMY: While it played in the corner of your screen.

Something happens.

JENN: Oh my God look.
AMY: Her face.
JENN: And his!
AMY: If it wasn't all so intense,
you could almost have [a giggle].

She laughs.

JENN: Oh my God.
AMY: Oh fuck.
JENN: Is he like just out of the shower or is he just fully sweating or …
AMY: Is that the number of people watching? Two hundred and two?
JENN: Yeah. This must be the moment. This is it!
AMY: Can you imagine, you know, fifteen years from now knowing that this is what your parents did online?
JENN: I think that's the top of the head?
AMY: That all these people watched this moment.
JENN: It's crowning.
AMY: Crowning?

JENN: Shall I turn the sound on?
AMY: No, no I don't think so.
My God she looks like she's in a lot of fucking pain, is she screaming?
JENN: Yeah, she's pushing a baby out.
AMY: It's so /
JENN: It's amazing.
AMY: There's a lot of other stuff coming out too.
JENN: Look we're at three hundred and sixty-seven.
AMY: Three seventy.
JENN: Oh my God we are about to witness this little being streamed into the world.
AMY: Alongside four hundred and twenty-one other people.
JENN: You want to bet on boy or girl?
AMY: What if there's an emergency?
JENN: I reckon a girl.
AMY: I mean fuck that would be bloody awful.
Us all in our homes watching something … God.
JENN: Look there's the head, the face.
AMY: It's looking up!
JENN: Posterior birth.
AMY: What's that?
JENN: Facing up. Little thing.
AMY: That's actually really freaking me out.
There's a head hanging out of her …
I'm minimising that right there.
JENN: The numbers are climbing …
AMY: Wow, little one, you have an audience of four hundred and eighty-nine people live at your birth.
Better smile.
JENN: It's got hair /
AMY: Five eighteen.
JENN: And its dad's nose!
AMY: There's a lot of freaking blood.
JENN: I wonder if it's the first Insta live birth during COVID?
AMY: I wonder if it is the first Insta live birth full stop!
JENN: Oh, she's pushing, look, look there's a shoulder.

AMY: I don't actually know this woman; I feel like a voyeur.
JENN: They have four other kids; this is nothing for them.
It's cool, an experiment.
Little thing look at that face.
AMY: Five hundred and thirty-nine wow it's like a virus, that curve is going through the roof.
JENN: Isn't it an amazing thing to be privy to.
On the next contraction the last shoulder will come out.
AMY: How well do you actually know the parents?
JENN: I went to primary school with her.
AMY: Bet you didn't know in grade one you'd be watching her push a baby out of her vagina via a thing called Instagram.
JENN: I didn't even know babies came out of vaginas at that age!
Look she's pushing.
AMY: Five hundred and eight-eight people watching. It's exciting.
JENN: Boy or girl?
AMY: I'll go for a boy.
JENN: Hang on.
AMY: What's happening?
JENN: Oh fuck!
AMY: What happened?
JENN: Quick let me try to get back on.
AMY: You're kidding me—get back on.
JENN: Oh shit. It's overloaded.
AMY: Overloaded? Is that a hospital phrase?
JENN: Bloody Instagram.
There's too many people streaming it live.
AMY: What, we can't get back on?
JENN: Hang on, I'm trying.
AMY: Wow, this baby just broke the internet.
It's almost a Kardashian and it's only got its head and one shoulder out!
JENN: Shit. Can't get back in!
AMY: No way! Is it a boy or girl?
JENN: No-one's writing, they're all watching.
AMY: You mean you have sat there all day through /
JENN: Eight hours of labour.

AMY: And then at the /
JENN: Fuck!
AMY: So you've been at a birth, watched the head come out, a shoulder; and then *bang*.
JENN: Fuck.
AMY: You don't even know …
JENN: Yeah. It's a bloody shame.
　　　Missed the most important bit.
AMY: The one thing everyone is going to ask you.
JENN: Huh?
AMY: Boy or girl?
JENN: Yeah.
AMY: You'll say, 'The birth was so beautiful', they'll say, 'Was it a boy or a girl?' and you'll say, 'Oh, I don't know, but it was such an amazing labour and birth'.
JENN: Yeah. Well it was.
AMY: It's kind of like a postmodern birth.
JENN: Little darling had a lot of hair.
AMY: The first non-gendered baby.
JENN: Dark hair too which is weird because they're both so fair.
AMY: A child of an era. A child of the future.
JENN: Fuck. You'd think someone would post about it.
AMY: They're all still in the room!
　　　Digitally lapping up the blood.
JENN: Not a single person is / posting
AMY: This is like watching the World Cup all the way through with no idea who won!
JENN: Well, somewhere over the other side of the world another person just came into being.
AMY: Yeah. Cool.
　　　Well, my meeting starts in five.
JENN: Shit, my wi-fi is cutting out.
AMY: Let me know when you hear …
　　　Jenn?
　　　Jenn?
　　　Okay.
　　　Well there you have it.

I'm talking to myself on Zoom.
Hello there.

Leans in.

Jesus, that hair colour. Time to head to a salon.
Minimise those freaking grey bits.

She peers at her face and fixes her hair.

Picks up her cold cup of tea.

Stands and leaves the room.

Suzie Miller
5 August 2020

NEARLY DARK

Jackson's suit is a lifeless shade of blue.
My dog isn't scared of him, she looks him in the eye.
Good girl, Tessa.
He prods, and the lights of consultation room making noises of insects.
The cat woman who failed to spark conversation with me in the waiting room, has succeeded with the vet nurse on the other side of the thin wall.
This crisis is biblical. There is little anyone can do to help except stay away, stay inside.
Her cat's pained meow.
You're alright, Mitzie. So I think we are all preparing, even subconsciously. Just like Noah did.
Jackson pats Tessa on the head and she looks up at him. Into his eyes.
Everyone's getting passengers for their arks.
That! I say. She looked at me. What she just did. She has never done that to me.
The vet seems puzzled.
How long have you had her?
Three weeks. Is she alright. She's not defective?
She's really healthy.
She must have looked at you.
No.
It has been three weeks, four days and eleven hours. Tess has not looked directly at me once.
Wherever we go other dogs retreat. It's always just Tessa and me.
Her looking away and me …
Here we are again, back in the socialising area; the dirt at the bottom of the hill which is just a big dog toilet.
Tessa sniffing at the tumbleweed as it blows across and back.
I watch the wind catch a plastic bag; it swirls and flies and gets dumped and reminds me of a scene in a film I forgot.
I had a picnic on this very hill a few years ago for my fortieth.

Was meant to be up the top but it had been taken.
I met Derek that day. Just over there, near that bush.
My celebrations always clash with the Grand Final so the turnout wasn't strong. That year it was on the actual day. I should have made it earlier but I pinned my hopes on some of the geeks who say they hate the footy. But even they came late and I got there early with so much to drink I had time to get miserable.
I needed to wee behind the bushes. Actually, I also needed to spew. So I was behind that bush when Derek appeared. He didn't seem to be worried about the smell.
Leaves look soft from here but they are not. Rub your skin against it and it can give you a nasty rash. Some plants.

>*She touches her skin and remembers.*

>*Picks up a stick, holds it up.*

Tessa! Here!
She turns and looks above me, slightly to the left.
Vet checked her sight.
Tessa!
Her sight is fine.

She doesn't like the frisbee or balls.

She's not into catching or chasing.
She likes to chew these beyond recognition. The remote controls, my old journals, the stuffed toy rabbit I've had since I was a girl. Chewed beyond recognition, added to the pile of debris.

I wish she could play cards. Or sweep floors.

>*A plane descends above her.*

She was a farm dog but that didn't work out.
They described her on the website as a quiet well-mannered girl in need of love. And I thought peas in a pod, you know.
On the way to the pound I knew that and wondered if it'd be obvious why. When they opened the cage at the pound, all the other dogs yapping away, she reeled back and yelped, my heart broke and like everything that I've ever got close to, I wanted to save her.

Driving back to the city she sat in the back of the car and stared out the window as a novelist might.

She'd never been inside a flat before. She stood at the front door staring at the floor boards as if she was a princess barefoot at the edge of a frozen lake.

Planes passing overhead terrified her.

Wait until they all come back into service. I whispered to her and she almost looked up at me but sighed instead. I don't think I imagined this: on that first day at the door, she kind of leant on my leg and let me stroke her head once. Her hair felt warm that first night.

She soon figured out the floorboards. And anything living under the flight path has no choice but to submit.

But she's not let me pat her since that night. I tried the next day but she moved away.

It can take months. To adjust. Jackson says.

To wag a tail. Doesn't she wonder why its dangling between her back legs?

My mum always said that if I got to a point in my life where I was worried about being alone, I should actually get the dog I have always talked about getting in this moment.

I wish she could have met Tess. She was good with dogs and kids.

It was sudden, poor Mum. Half-done puzzle sitting on her kitchen table like a riddle. Was it for the best? Would she have coped with isolation as immunity?

I miss her most on Sundays. She always cheated on the quiz in the paper. Swore to me she hadn't looked at the answers.

She used to say, *your biggest strength is that you're empathetic.*

I wonder if she knew there's no such a word?

Tessa?

She does her own thing and makes me wait. I wish she'd play with the other dogs.

I took some pictures of her to keep. In the photos her eyes are red like the devil's.

This park got so dead. Nobody's going out, when I call people they are all on Zoom, when I Zoom them they are all on the phone.

Do dogs sense what's going on?

Tessa? Tessa?

Tessa?
Nothing.
Looks like it might rain. I'll go up the hill so I can look down and find her.
I don't panic. Having a dog is not about inducing panic.
It's about fun.
Black bags full of fun.
Fun expenses and fun apologies to neighbours and a future full of new fun people.
Tessa?
There she is. Being pursued by a big dog who gains on her. The kind of dog that should be pulling a sleigh not catching ticks here. A dog with big teeth and a nose like a horse that sniffs between Tessa's back legs.
Big pink tongue like a fat side of ham. Penis a decisive ruby arrow between his legs.
Tessa?
He's mounting her. Is she in this?
Tess?
Who owns this fucking dog?
Tessa?
Nobody appears with a lead. There is nobody else. I scream at the dog,
You rapist!
I run at it shouting. *Leave her alone. She's fragile, she has no defences she's ...*
And as I get closer Tessa turns and looks at me and gives me a back-off look.
Tessa?
She growls.
I back away.
The big dog licks his lips, finishes and goes on his way.
Tessa looks at me again with a gleam in her eye.
Rain spits on the dirt.
It's nearly dark, come on.

Lachlan Philpott
30 August 2020

AND I'M HERE

And I'm here, on the edge.
My face to the ocean, the river behind
The city, old, new, this place, this home, this space

Air so clean so cold I could drink it

The smiling started the day after
The day after it all began
Just a half-hour walk through the street
past house after house of friendly neighbours
Caring cats and docile dogs and teddy bears left in windows for children to point at on their one-hour exercise. Put up in the first lockdown, left there for the second.

At the start we tried to be jolly about everything
Smiling at lovely neighbours
Glass of wine
on our deckchairs
On the pavement
Out by the letterbox
Social distancing of course
On the driveway
By the carport
Winter came
And once we had a little fire in a brazier, provided by a lovely neighbour, two doors up
Glass of wine

As time passed
It started to seem
Well, there's only so many glasses of chardonnay you can drink
Plus the cold and the weather.
We tried to be neighbourly
Really
We gave each other garden flowers
And seeds

THE CURVE

And firewood
And books to read
And recipes to make
Herbs
And offers of lifts to the supermarket
And doctor's appointments
But after a while
It stopped
All that feeling just seeped out
It went back to the way it always was
Except it was worse
Because we should have been
We could have been
The concrete footpath cracked and the council were informed.
Two Doors Up had a seizure during the night and nearly bit her tongue in half and she drove herself to the hospital
Someone stole the kids bikes next door
Him Across The Road had one of his psychotic episodes and we all stop at our windows and watch the flashing lights of the police car.

It's spring now
The magpies are out, picking at insects, swooping and clacking their beaks

Council re-cemented the footpath and all the kids waited till the men were gone and then rushed out with bits of stick and stone and wrote their names in thick wet concrete.

And we wear masks because
Well
they say it protects us from the virus
But really
it stops all that goddamned
smiling.

Vanessa Bates
1 September 2020

SHINE

It's December 26, 1992. Merry Christmas for yesterday. I am twenty. I wake up in my childhood bedroom not knowing then that I will never sleep in here again.
In the kitchen, Dad slyly unwraps the pillowcase encasing the ham. The ham slip. It smells like Dad's pillow; rank from nightlong summerlong sweat and all the ham he is processing.
He's hacks a huge pink hunk off and shoves it in his mouth. Protective of what's left, he quickly wraps it again while gobbling. This is how it will go until nothing's left but the bone.
Ham turns Dad into a starving dog.
You're up early.
He nods. His mouth too full to speak.
I have never understood why he is sly with ham. He paid for it. He likes it so much why shouldn't he eat the lot?
Are you bringing me coffee?
Mum's tired voice from the lounge room.
And a bit of cold turkey?
Dad is the Ham King and his wife is Turkey Queen.
My brother is a custard guzzler and tongue poker of the Chinaman's belly; his name for the yellow skin that forms on top when it's taken off the stove.
After being a fat teenager who only watched others pash at parties, I went on a diet that I am still on. It does not include meat, so when it comes to leftovers, my family are thrilled I'm out.
You can have all the sprouts.
I am also a champion bulimic. There are lots of ways to lose weight but this way has become a fine-tuned ritual of life for me now—a kind of late-teen obsession.
People compliment me on how well I have done becoming slim and I blush and say little, even if I want to tell them how right they are. I have done so well I haven't kept an entire meal down since 1989. I'm sly in a way that shows off its genetic evolution. My sly is so much better than my dad's sly.
I go to kiss Mum on the cheek but bulimic balance means I miss and

kiss the edge of her starchy towelling robe instead.
Mum's hand tenderly cups a decoration that must have fallen in the night. The little brown pup in a stocking.
Falling apart.
Can he be mended? I ask.
The once-green nettles on the tree are turning brown.
There is birdcall, then silence, then more birdcall.
You okay? Mum squeezes my hand.
Dad whistles in the kitchen and the kettle builds momentum to join him.
Me? Yeah of course, I'm great.
Teaspoons clatter.
But there is something I ...
This is my moment.
Mum waits.
Say it now; take a big breath and do it ...
So ... I'm in love.
Watch Mum's reflection on a bauble. Her smile fades after I say:
With a man.
Her grip on dog in the stocking tightens.
Dad takes a sip of trusty Nescafe and nods his head, ready to hear more, look on his face like I tell him this kind of stuff every morning. Mum glares at him and then out the window at the neighbour busy poisoning her weeds.
In this moment I am surprised. I have always assumed Mum knew me. There were so many signs. My obsessive use of both grandmother's hand-me-down nighties and frocks, my disdain for cricket, cubs and camping, my obsession with Tiffany and shopping malls. How did mother reconcile her frequent discovery of old carrots or candles under my bed? This being the same place she found a can of deodorant with poo and blood on one end.
This wasn't the era where claiming difference was easy. Celebrating uniqueness was less popular than dobbing where I grew up. Being gay, like, actually gay was unheard of. There were no gays living in French's Forest.
My parents were accepting and open-minded compared to others I

knew. They were educated, voted left and involved in theatre. They played Elton John. When it's your kid, well it is clearly a different matter.

What happened next was the same thing that happened for many of the gays of my generation.

Mum stares hard and in a soft voice says:

You'll get AIDS.

I don't remember what got said next.

From what my brother tells me tinsel was torn, fairy lights ripped, and nobody has spoken about the dog in the stocking since.

In the tearing, a nervous bauble shattered and cut the palms of her hands; her blood stained the good carpet in the good room.

Is that stain her fault or mine? She broke her bauble and it was her blood that dripped. But it was my news.

Is her blood mine? Our blood?

It is our blood that stains the carpet but it's my blood that will surely get infected with the virus and it will be my life cut short. Is that my fault?

She repeats and adds my name at the end;

You will die from AIDS, Lachlan.

The tone is more certain this time. Mothers know. They have some access to a crystal ball that shows so many young gay men's lives will be held ransom by HIV and that a large proportion of them will test positive. Without medication, HIV will develop into AIDS and lead to death. Maybe she knows this because it is the story of 1982 and 1983 and 1984 and 1985 and 1986 and 1987 and 1988 and 1989 and 1990 and 1991 and 1992 and now …

The bauble's broken, the fairy lights fucked. Her firstborn child is a faggot. The sand in his hourglass slip-slides away.

What will it be for her after that? How will she face all the shame? This is the unthinkable loss of the young and invincible as had only been experienced in wartimes. And with it comes panic and blame and a quest to distance oneself from it and all that it means.

Mum's first words echo in my head every day for decades after.

A constant shadow; every step, every glance, every kiss.

Fear was served out so generously.

I did my best to prove Mum wrong but we all slip up. In 1996, I knew I had been exposed. I felt such deep shame and couldn't tell anyone. After forty-eight hours panicking, I went to the clinic at Sydney Hospital.

Take one tablet every four hours, even during the night. The side effects should settle after a week or two. Whatever you do, don't miss a dose.

At that time PEP was AZT. It made me shit like a flash flood about fifteen minutes after I had taken it. When that and a change of undies was done, a stabbing headache began. The headache lasted another hour which gave me about two hours before the cycle started again. The side effects did not wear off. I know this story is nothing compared to those who were on AZT hoping that more effective medication would arrive before it was too late but this is my story.

It's 2020. I am masked in the park meeting a very close friend for a masked socially distanced walk. In the space of this walk, my friend quizzes me on how many people I am 'seeing' in this manner. I tell them four others and they step back and say;

I think I need to put things with us on hold until ...

'Things with us?' You mean a masked walk outside where the wind is blowing during which you ensure we never get closer than one point five metres.

They do mean this.

Are you saying you consider me hazardous?

This triggers me in a way that takes me back to 1996. I shake as I turn and walk home, alone.

How many times did this sort of thing play out during COVID?

At least those who contracted COVID didn't get called COVID carriers. Were they spat on in the street or evicted? Did a gang of teens hunt down the couple who started the Avalon cluster and make them choose between jumping off the cliffs at Barrenjoey Head or being pushed over instead?

Did you hear anyone say *I needn't worry about COVID because it is only really the old that die?*

Like COVID, in the early days, nobody knew what HIV was or how it was being passed on. In order to keep the population safe, nations all around the world undertook rigid lockdowns, right?

The arts, especially ballet companies and shops selling items like glitter, disco supplies, leather cleaner and actual leather were in real trouble. So, the government of the day offered a stimulus package that can easily be seen as the early version blueprint of Jobkeeper. Not.

But they made condoms available at large dance parties and bath houses and there were quarantines much like the ones tennis players have recently complained about just not in hotel rooms. Isolated parts of hospitals and cold isolated cells were the go then.

When a disease threatens a demographic, governments make tough decisions. Protecting children from measles or polio makes sense. When it comes to protecting the most robust contributors—groups of young adults—why does it get blurry?

The world may be kinder than it was back then but this seems unlikely. Did we become more humane because of the blinding neglect and mishandling of HIV? Was the sacrifice made by that population worth what we get now?

Vanessa Amorosi is a singer with an amazing voice who cannot dance. Despite this, she could have become a gay icon if her target audience weren't so busy dropping dead. The chorus of her most enduring song originally went:

Look around you
Everyone you see
Everyone you know
Is going to *die*.
Yes. Die.

But someone along the line sorted this out and changed the lyrics. *Die* became shine.

And the song of stolen truth became the hit of Sydney's Paralympic Games.

We don't enjoy talking about death.

It spoils life. After spoiling that Boxing Day, I'm hesitant to go a-spoiling again.

But why in fuck is absolutely everybody nostalgically raiding the '80s right now? Even the most terrible school bullies' mullets are back on new heads.

The '80s was not the era we think it was. Gen X know this, and I know nobody cares about us but this might be something you need to hear.
The '80s was as cold as the war that raged on in it. A time when turning your back was the biggest move of the era, not the moonwalk. A move that even kind, generous, funny mothers mastered.
Charles began it by turning his back on Camilla then Diana. America turned its back on sanity and voted Reagan in. Nuclear accidents, microwave dinners, greenhouse gasses, famines, assassinations, walls coming down, and revolutions with people standing in the way of tanks and shot down in broad daylight. There was so much to ignore that turning away was for the best.
The past should haunt us here in Australia because we invaders have been a mob of cunts. But there is no point feeling guilty about the past unless we understand what we did.
So let's stop that inherited guilt stuff and examine the truth of what actually happened.
Dig a little. It's down there waiting for the light to shine on it.
Ready? Start with your family.
Was being honest about who I am worth being told that by your mother?
Yes.
My secret eating disorder ended when I came out. I was too busy taking precautions against HIV to be running off the loo to chuck.
Did the precautions I took work?
Whether I ended up getting it or not is not the point.
Do you know if you can get COVID from a toilet seat or a coffee cup? How about HIV?
Whatever the answer is, something will shine.
We will all shine. Every single one of us.
Vanessa knew that and wrote her song.
You know it.
I know it.
Shine!

Lachlan Philpott
4 February 2021

CRITICAL STAGES TOURING

presents

THE CURVE

28 APRIL, 2021

Writers
**Vanessa Bates, Mary Rachel Brown, Suzie Miller,
Lachlan Philpott and Katie Pollock**

Director
Chris Bendall

Production Manager
Lucy Dinh

Performers
**Kip Chapman
Laurence Coy
Katrina Foster
Aileen Huynh
Lucia Mastrantone
Sam Wang**

For Critical Stages Touring
Senior Producer **Melanie Carolan**
Programming Producer **Emma Corrick**
Marketing and Engagment **Robbi James**
Creative Producer **Bernadette Fam**
Production Supervisor **Judy Reardon**
Finance Manager **Kylie Richards**

Critical Stages Touring would like to acknowledge the premiere production was rehearsed and performed on Gadigal Country, and to extend our respect to Elders of this land.

This project was supported by the City of Sydney, Create NSW, the Russell Mills Foundation, and the Australian Government through the Australia Council for the Arts, its arts funding and advisory body.

DIRECTOR'S NOTE

This is a remarkable collection of writing from five outstanding playwrights, whose work I have long admired. Each writer has interrogated the unique times we have been living through with remarkable depth, warmth, humour and hope. I feel immensely privileged to have the opportunity to bring these short works to the stage for the first time. I am very grateful to be working with such an outstanding cast to give voice to their stories and to share them with audiences both live and virtual.

The Curve will also be an exciting addition to our new CST Screening Room, and creates an ideal companion piece to our *Come To Where I Am Australia* series, profiling the work of outstanding Australian playwrights to tell the story of these unforgettable times.

Thank you to Vanessa, Katie, Lachlan, Mary and Suzie for your trust and collaboration and to all my production team at Critical Stages Touring for helping to make this possible. I would also like to acknowledge our crucial government and philanthropic partners who have made this all possible.

I do hope you enjoy.

—Chris Bendall
8 April 2021

VANESSA BATES
WRITER

Vanessa is an award-winning playwright (NSW Premiers Literary Award and most recently 2019 AWGIE Award for Theatre for Young Audiences) and screenwriter. Plays include *A Ghost In My Suitcase (the play)*, *Trailer*, *Light Begins To Fade*, *Every Second*, *The Magic Hour*, *PORN.CAKE*, *Checklist For An Armed Robber* and *Darling Oscar*. Television includes *EastWest 101* (SBS), *Rush* (Channel 10), *Play School* (ABCTV), *Twentyfourseven* (SBS) and the ABCTV feature-length documentary *900 Neighbours*. Short films include *Pop's Dream* and *The HoneyEaters*. For television, Vanessa is currently working with Ross Mueller to write two comedy drama series; *lovelife* (Princess Pictures) and *Troubled Youth*. Currently commissioned by Sydney's Ensemble Theatre to write a new play for 2022, *The One*, about the Asian/Eurasian Australian identity, Vanessa has been produced at Malthouse Theatre, Barking Gecko, Sydney Theatre Company, Darlinghurst Theatre, Black Swan Theatre, Griffin, Deckchair, Theatre@Risk, atyp, Tantrum and many others. She is a playwrighting mentor/teacher, an AWG Playwrights Committee member, a NIDA Playwrights Studio graduate and one seventh of playwrights' company 7ON. She is also completing a PhD in Scriptwriting.

MARY RACHEL BROWN
WRITER

Mary is the recipient of the following Playwriting Awards: The Lysicrates Prize, The Rodney Seaborn Playwright's Award, The Max Afford Playwright's Award, and The Griffin Award. Mary was a writer on *Betty Blokk Buster Reimagined* for the 2020 Sydney Festival. Her most recent play *Dead Cat Bounce* opened Griffin Theatre Company's 2019 season. Mary's most notable work, *The Dapto Chaser*, was commissioned by Merrigong and reproduced by Apocalypse Theatre for Griffin Independent, Glenn St and Hothouse. The play was screened at Dendy Cinemas and on ABC iview as part of Australian Theatre Live's program. Other works for the stage include *All My Sleep and Waking* (Apocalypse Theatre), *Permission to Spin* (Apocalypse Theatre), *Inside Out* (Christine Dunstan Productions) and *Die Fledermaus* (Adaption) (Sydney Conservatorium of Music). TV credits include sketch writing for *The Elegant Gentleman's Guide to Knife Fighting* for ABC and several episodes of *Home and Away* for Chanel 7.

SUZIE MILLER
WRITER

Suzie graduated as a playwright from the NIDA Playwrights' Studio 2000, and is a contemporary international playwright, screenwriter and librettist, drawn to complex human stories often exploring injustice. Miller's plays have had 40 productions around the world winning multiple prestigious awards including: 2020 AWGIE for Drama; 2020 David Williamson Award for Outstanding Theatre Writing; the 2020 prestigious over all categories AWGIE; the Kit Denton Award for writing with courage (2009); NY Fringe Excellence in Writing Award 2008 and more. She has been commissioned by, or been in residence at, multiple prestigious theatres including London's National Theatre, the National Theatre of Scotland, Theatre Gargantua Canada, and in Australia with Malthouse Theatre, La Boite Theatre and Griffin Theatre, and a creative fellow with the University of Qld. Miller's most recent and forthcoming productions span London's West End, NY Broadway, Sydney, Melbourne and Brisbane. She is contracted to write a number of international screenplays for film and TV (with Bunya Australia, Hoodlum, Matchbox Pictures/NBC, Film Art Media and numerous US producers). Suzie has a background in both science and law, is primarily based in both Sydney and London and is represented by HLA Sydney; David Higham and Associates London.

LACHLAN PHILPOTT
WRITER

Lachlan has created an extensive body of texts that provoke people to listen and challenge the perspectives through which we see and remember. He writes to bear witness to the small details, big questions, contradictions and vanishing integrities so common in these times. His plays for young audiences have been widely performed and awarded. He has also collaborated with Dr Alyson Campbell for over 20 years under the banner wreckedALLprods in work documenting the evolving lives of his queer family. Lachlan initiated Australian Theatre for Young People's Emerging Writers' Program and his teaching and mentorship have nurtured many young writers in theatre companies, schools and universities in Australia and internationally. He was Artistic Director/CEO of Playwriting Australia and Tantrum. He has been in residence at La Comedie Francaise, Kansas State University, The American Conservatory Theatre, Griffin, The Playwrights Foundation, Red Stitch and The Traverse. Chair of the AWG playwrights committee (2012-2015), Lachlan was the inaugural Australian Professional Playwright Fulbright Scholar.

KATIE POLLOCK
WRITER

Katie is an award-winning Sydney-based playwright. Her plays for theatre are *Normal*; *The Becoming*; *The Hansard Monologues (Age of Entitlement)*; *Blue Italian/Nil by Sea*; *The Hansard Monologues (A Matter of Public Importance)*; *The Blue Angel Hotel*; *A Quiet Night in Rangoon*; *A Girl Called Red*; and numerous short works. Her plays and adaptations for radio are *Beetroot: A bloody journey through roots and belonging*; *Nil by Sea*; *Contact*; *O is for Oxygen*; and *Blue Italian*. Her works have been produced by ABC Radio, Apocalypse Theatre, Canberra Youth Theatre, Casula Powerhouse, Eastside FM, Hothouse

Theatre, Merrigong Theatre, Museum of Australian Democracy, New Theatre, Newtown Theatre, Old 505 Theatre, Redline Productions, Seymour Centre, Site and Sound Festival, subtlenuance, Sydney Fringe Festival, Tamarama Rock Surfers and The Street. Awards include the Rodney Seaborn Playwrights Award, the Martin Lysicrates Prize, the inaugural Town Hall Theatre (USA) 'Ingenious' award, the Inscription/Edward Albee Playwriting Scholarship, the Australian Writers Guild's What Happens Next prize, Hothouse Theatre's Solo competition and three AWGIE nominations. She has plays in development with Merrigong Theatre Company, The Street and Bakehouse Theatre at KXT. She has been a proud member of the Australian Writers Guild since 2009. *Normal* is published by Currency Press.

CHRIS BENDALL
DIRECTOR

Chris is an award-winning arts leader, artistic director, programmer, producer, playwright and dramaturg. He has been Director and CEO of Critical Stages Touring since 2014, creating outstanding professional theatre and live performance experiences for regional and metropolitan audiences across Australia and New Zealand. Previous positions include: Artistic Director and CEO of Deckchair Theatre in Fremantle WA; Guest Curator of the 2013 National Play Festival for Playwriting Australia; Artistic Director of Theatre@Risk in Melbourne, Affiliate Director at Melbourne Theatre Company; Founding Committee Member andTreasurer of Theatre Network NSW; and Chair of Stages WA. Directing highlights include: Vanessa Bates' *The Magic Hour* (National Tour 2014 including Queensland Theatre, Darwin Festival and finalist for APACA's Drover Award for Tour of the Year); Marie Jones' *Stones in his Pockets* (NSW tours 2015-2016 and National Tour 2017); Reg Cribb's *Thomas Murray and the Upside-Down River* (Griffin Theatre and NORPA 2016, National Tour 2018); Robert

Drewe's *Grace* adapted for the stage by Humphrey Bower (Perth International Arts Festival 2010); Vanessa Bates' *Checklist for an Armed Robber* (Deckchair Theatre and Theatre@Risk Melbourne); *7 Days 10 Years* by Louis Milutinovic (winner of Green Room Award Best New Play); and Noëlle Janaczewska's *Mrs Petrov's Shoe* (winner of QLD Premier's Literary Award Best New Play). Chris has also worked for Melbourne Theatre Company, Playbox Theatre, Belvoir St Theatre and Sydney Theatre Company. Chris twice won the WA Equity Award for Best Director and Best Production (2009, 2011); and was nominated for a Victorian Green Room Award for Outstanding Direction (2001). He has been awarded the Queen's Trust Australia and Foundation for Young Australians Centenary Grant (2001) and the George Fairfax Memorial Award for Theatre (2003). Critical Stages Touring won the PAC Australia Touring Legend Award for 2019.

LUCY DINH
PRODUCTION MANAGER

Moonlighting as a production manager one day, then as a lighting technician the next, Lucy is experienced in logistical and technical aspects of production, having worked as an event technician, music events coordinator, and production coordinator at UNSW (2016–present). Throughout the year, she also works with various other arts companies, taking part in lighting installations such as on the Sydney Harbour Bridge, and for the Night Noodle Markets; and in the production of major events including Vivid, Sydney Festival and Sydney New Year's Eve.

KIP CHAPMAN
PERMFORMER

In 2013 Kip was a recipient of the New Zealand Arts Foundation New Generation Award for services to theatre. Stage highlights include lead roles in: *Equus, Lobby Hero, Big River, The Goat, Little Dog Laughed, The Pride, Black Confetti, The Caretaker, The Glass Menagerie* and *Hudson & Halls*. Other work includes: *The Talented Mr Ripley, Flagons and Foxtrots, Romeo and Juliet, The Mooncake and The Kumara, Famous Flora, Sex with Strangers, Macbeth, Hamlet, Play 2, Rise and Fall of Little Voice* (Darlinghurst Theatre Company) and *Kasama Kita* (Belvoir Downstairs). Screen highlights include: *Top of the Lake* and *The Lord of the Rings* (TV Series).

LAURENCE COY
PERFORMER

As an actor on stage, Laurence has worked for all Australia's State Theatre Companies, Bell Shakespeare, Belvoir St, Perth, Adelaide and Sydney Festivals, Monkey Baa, Hayes Theatre Co, and many commercial and independent producers. His feature film credits include *Ladies In Black, San Andreas, The Chronicles of Narnia: Voyage of the Dawn Treader, Fool's Gold, The Three Stooges* and *Doing Time For Patsy Cline*. On television he has appeared in *Devil's Dust, Wild Boys, Rake, Crownies* and *Paper Giants: The Birth of Cleo*. He is a graduate in Theatre Studies from UNSW, in Acting from WAAPA, in Directing from NIDA, and in Screenwriting from UTS.

KATRINA FOSTER
PERFORMER

Since graduating from NIDA, Katrina has worked as an actor across all mediums including theatre, film and television. Most recently she completed a national tour of *I Want to Know What Love Is* with Queensland-based The Good Room and will be performing again in the show at Sydney's Darlinghurst Theatre in 2021. Before that she appeared in *Dream Home*, directed by David Williamson, for Ensemble Theatre in Sydney and in *Mum's the Word* and *Mum's the Word II: Teenagers*, both playing to audiences across Australia. She has worked across all states, for all major theatre companies, including Sydney Theatre Company, Melbourne Theatre Company, Ensemble Theatre, Griffin Theatre, Belvoir, Queensland Theatre and State Theatre Company of South Australia. Her television credits include *Rake*, *Sea Change* and *All Saints*. She has also worked as a television writer and script editor for many years. as well as a dramaturg and lecturer in scriptwriting, dramaturgy and storytelling.

AILEEN HUYNH
PERFORMER

A graduate from WAAPA, you will regularly find Aileen treading the boards on Australian stages. She was recently in David Williamson's world premiere of *The Big Time* at Ensemble Theatre, playing the ambitious and feisty Kendra in Branden Jacob-Jenkins' Pulitzer nominated *Gloria* for The Melbourne Theatre Company, and Julian Larnach's *Flight Paths* for The National Theatre of Parramatta. She has done national tours of *4000 Miles* (Critical Stages) and *Hello Goodbye & Happy Birthday* (Performing Lines), which received a Helpmann nomination. Aileen made her screen debut in the critically acclaimed SBS mini-series *Better Man*. Since then her screen credits have included *Neighbours*, *Black Comedy 3*, *The Commons* and as mad scientist Everick in series 1&2 of *Cleverman*. As a content creator she has worked independently on short comedy skit videos and was nominated in 2014 for an Australian Online Video Award. Shortly after she worked with comedy legends Tim Ferguson and Marc Gracie on their feature film *Spin Out*. Her current content work can be seen on YouTube under her alter ego Dr Mad Phan. In 2019 she made her directorial debut with Sam Wang's comedy stage show

Skyduck: A Chinese Spy Comedy with Belvoir 25a. It received two honourable mentions for 'Best of 2019 on stage in Sydney' in Timeout and Audrey Journal.

LUCIA MASTRANTONE
PERFORMER

Lucia has a successful career in theatre, physical theatre, film, TV and as a voice artist. She recently performed in *Young Frankenstein* as the legendary 'Frau Blucher' for The Hayes. Other recent credits include *The Harp in the South Parts 1 and 2*, *Talk*, *Marriage Blanc*, *Romeo and Juliet* (Sydney Theatre Company), *Dead Cat Bounce*, *Kill Climate Deniers*, *Ladies Day* (Griffin), *Atlantis*, *Twelfth Night*, *Scorched* (Belvoir), *The Hypochondriac* (Darlinghurst Theatre), and *Blue Love* (Shaun Parker Dance Co). Lucia featured in TV series *Tangle*, *Rake*, *The Letdown*, *Home and Away* and the AFI Award-winning films *Look Both Ways*, *Bad Boy Bubby* and co-starred in Working Dog's hit animation *Pacific Heat*.

SAM WANG
PERFORMER

Sam studied filmmaking and law at the University of Technology, Sydney before training as an actor at Toi Whakaari: New Zealand Drama School. On screen, his acting credits include *Life is Easy* (TVNZ OnDemand), *Hope & Wire* (TVNZ), *Runaway Millionaires* (Channel 7) and he will be appearing soon in *New Gold Mountain* (SBS). His stage credits include *The Mooncake & The Kumara* (Kia Mau Festival) and *The Chairs: Cantonese Season* (Te Rēhia Theatre). In 2019, Sam premiered his solo comedy stage show, *Skyduck: A Chinese Spy Comedy*, which earnt him a nomination at the Sydney Theatre Awards. He also won the South Pacific Picture's Big Pitch Competition for his half-hour comedy, *HomeBound 3.0*, which is currently being developed with Kevin & Co. Sam practiced law for several years and also holds a Master of Commerce (Finance) from the University of New South Wales.

CRITICAL STAGES TOURING

Critical Stages Touring is Australia's national touring theatre company—discovering and commissioning outstanding independent theatre for audiences everywhere. We create experiences that connect communities across a national network of over 100 theatres and presenting partners; support sector development through industry support initiatives like the Indy Theatre Forums and our Stage & Stream guides; and now connect local artists with the world through the development of original works for the CST Screening Room, our new online platform for digital theatre.

Our vision is to enable regional communities to have the same access to high quality theatre as audiences with access to metropolitan storytellers. We identify and develop innovative touring productions, deliver impactful live performance opportunities to diverse communities nationally, and play a leading role in the development of a vibrant and resilient independent theatre sector. Since our formation in 2005, we have been touring outstanding theatrical experiences right across Australia and New Zealand.

In 2019 Critical Stages Touring was the recipient of the prestigious 2019 Drovers Touring Legend Award.

For more information head to: www.criticalstages.com.au

www.currency.com.au

Visit Currency Press' website now to:

- Order books
- Browse through our full list of titles including plays, screenplays, theory and reference/criticism, performance handbooks, educational texts and more
- Choose a play for your school or performance group by cast specs
- Seek performance rights
- Find out about performing arts news and sign up for our newsletter
- For students: read our study guides
- For teachers: access free curriculum information and teacher notes

We are also on Facebook and Instagram (@currencypress). Join the conversation!

The performing arts publisher

www.ingramcontent.com/pod-product-compliance
Lightning Source LLC
Chambersburg PA
CBHW042131160426
43198CB00022B/2973